PENGUIN TWENTIETH-CENTURY CLASSICS
COMPLETE POEMS

As an educator, lawyer, newspaper publisher, poet, lyricist, diplomat, novelist, and champion for human rights, James Weldon Johnson contributed greatly to American life and world culture.

Born in Jacksonville, Florida, in 1871, to James and Helen Louise Dillet Johnson, he graduated from Atlanta University in 1894, where he was valedictorian. That same year he was appointed principal of Stanton School in Jacksonville. In 1896 he made Stanton the first public high school for blacks in the state of Florida. The following year he founded the *Daily American*, a daily newspaper serving Jacksonville's black population, and became the first African American to pass the Florida bar.

Johnson moved to New York in 1902 to form the musical trio, Cole and the Johnson Brothers. During the first years of the twentieth century, the trio had all America singing "Congo Love Song," "Under the Bamboo Tree," and "Sence You Went Away." With the trio, Johnson went on to write the lyrics of more than 200 songs and, with Irving Berlin, Victor Herbert, and John Philip Sousa, he founded the American Society of Composers, Authors and Publishers (ASCAP). A United States diplomat in South and Central America from 1906 to 1913, he returned to New York and became editor of the black weekly newspaper, *The New York Age*.

After joining the staff of the National Association for the Advancement of Colored People in 1916, he became its chief executive officer in 1920, serving in that capacity for a decade. As an NAACP official, Johnson is credited for making the organization nationally visible, enlarging its membership, and mounting an unprecedented national campaign against lynching.

A prolific writer, his books include *Fifty Years and Other Poems, The Autobiography of an Ex-Colored Man, The Book of American Negro Poetry, The Books of American Negro Spirituals, Along This Way: An Autobiography, Black Manhattan, Saint Peter Relates an Incident: Selected Poems, God's Trombones: Seven Negro Sermons in Verse,* and *Negro Americans, What Now?*

He died on June 26, 1938, as a result of an automobile accident in Wiscassett, Maine. At the time of his death he was serving as professor of creative literature at Fisk University and professor of Negro literature at New York University.

Dr. Sondra Kathryn Wilson, executor of James Weldon Johnson's literary properties, is an associate of the W. E. B. Du Bois Institute at Harvard University. Her publications include two volumes of *The Selected Writings of James Weldon Johnson* (1995); *In Search of Democracy* (1999); *The Crisis Reader* (1999); *Opportunity Reader* (1999); and *The Messenger Reader* (2000). With Julian Bond she co-edited *Lift Every Voice and Sing: 100 Years, 100 Voices* (2000).

JAMES WELDON JOHNSON
COMPLETE POEMS

JAMES WELDON JOHNSON
COMPLETE POEMS

EDITED WITH AN INTRODUCTION BY
SONDRA KATHRYN WILSON

PENGUIN BOOKS

AL BR

PS3519
.O2625
A17
2000

PENGUIN BOOKS
Published by the Penguin Group
Penguin Putnam Inc., 375 Hudson Street,
New York, New York 10014, U.S.A.
Penguin Books Ltd, 27 Wrights Lane,
London W8 5TZ, England
Penguin Books Australia Ltd, Ringwood,
Victoria, Australia
Penguin Books Canada Ltd, 10 Alcorn Avenue,
Toronto, Ontario, Canada M4V 3B2
Penguin Books (N.Z.) Ltd, 182–190 Wairau Road,
Auckland 10, New Zealand

Penguin Books Ltd, Registered Offices:
Harmondsworth, Middlesex, England

First published in Penguin Books 2000

1   3   5   7   9   10   8   6   4   2

Copyright The Viking Press, Inc., 1927
Copyright James Weldon Johnson, 1935
Copyright renewed Grace Nail Johnson, 1955, 1963
Copyright © Sondra Kathryn Wilson, Literary Executor of the Estate of
James Weldon Johnson, 2000
All rights reserved

LIBRARY OF CONGRESS CATALOGING IN PUBLICATION DATA
Johnson, James Weldon, 1871–1938.
[Poems]
Complete poems / James Weldon Johnson ; edited with an
introduction by Sondra Kathryn Wilson.
p. cm.
Includes bibliographical references.
ISBN 0 14 11.8545 7
1. Afro-Americans—Poetry.   I. Wilson, Sondra K.   II. Title.
PS3519.O2625 A17 2000
811′.52—dc21   00-039969

Printed in the United States of America
Set in Sabon

Except in the United States of America, this book is sold subject to the
condition that it shall not, by way of trade or otherwise, be lent, re-sold,
hired out, or otherwise circulated without the publisher's prior consent in
any form of binding or cover other than that in which it is published and
without a similar condition including this condition being imposed on the
subsequent purchaser.

To the memory of Grace Elizabeth Nail Johnson
(1885–1976)

CONTENTS

CONTENTS

INTRODUCTION

NAACP OFFICIALS HOSTED a black-tie dinner in the elegant ballroom of the Hotel Pennsylvania in New York City on the evening of Thursday, May 14, 1931, to honor James Weldon Johnson upon his retirement as leader of the civil rights organization. This affair, probably the most remarkable of its kind in the 1930s, included a diverse gathering of many of the most distinguished and talented people from practically every professional community in America. The power of Johnson's personality and the range of his achievements were commemorated by those who came to honor him by the moving tributes they paid. The literary critic Carl Van Doren said of the guest of honor: "He is an alchemist—he transformed baser metals into gold." Johnson had indeed used his brilliance and blackness to transform some of the most obscure expressions of black culture through literature. He elevated and brought those aspects of the black experience into American life and world culture.

One of the best representations of Johnson as an "alchemist" is his most famous work: *God's Trombones: Seven Negro Sermons in Verse*, published in 1927. As Henry Louis Gates, Jr., has written, "*God's Trombones*, alone, would have ensured Johnson's place in the canon." In this collection of poems, Johnson revealed to the world the creative genius of the unlettered black preachers. These old-time sermonizers were shunned and rebuked even by many of their own race. Johnson understood that many African Americans were ashamed of the so-called ignorant preacher and his exhortations. He explained this in his preface to the work:

> The old-time Negro preacher has not yet been given the niche in which he properly belongs. He has been portrayed as a semi-comic figure. He had, it is true, his comic aspects, but on the whole he was an important figure, and at bottom a vital factor.

The following are some lines from the sermon "The Prodigal Son" in *God's Trombones*:

Young man—
Young man—
Your arm's too short to box with God
But Jesus spake in a parable, and he said:
A certain man had two sons
Jesus didn't give this man a name,
But his name is God Almighty.
And Jesus didn't call these sons by name,
But ev'ry young man,
Ev'rywhere,
Is one of these two sons . . .

Johnson transformed the folk sermons of the old-time preacher into beautiful and inspiring poetry. By preserving a race's oral history, he single-handedly made these powerful sermons an important part of American literature.

We can also easily see Johnson as an "alchemist" in his *Books of American Negro Spirituals*. In this seminal work, initially published in two volumes (1925, 1926), Johnson adroitly delineates the origin, artistic character, and historical significance of the spirituals. The renowned poet Carl Sandburg described Johnson's interpretation of this African-American art form as "the best statement and explanation of the singing of the spirituals that I have ever seen." Johnson wrote about the creative genius of the slaves in his poem "O Black and Unknown Bards":

O Black and unknown bards of long ago,
How came your lips to touch the sacred fire?
How, in your darkness, did you come to know
The power and beauty of the minstrel's lyre?
Who first from midst his bonds lifted his eyes?
Who first from out the still watch, lone and long?
Feeling the ancient faith of prophets rise
Within his dark-kept soul, burst into song?

Heart of what slave poured out such melody
As "Steal Away to Jesus"? on its strains

His spirit must have nightly floated free,
Though still about his hands he felt his chains.
Who heard great "Jordan Roll"? . . .

Johnson reveals in "O Black and Unknown Bards" African Americans as creators of the Negro spirituals who lived and died captives of a system of slave labor. He wrote pointedly, "But from whom did these songs spring—these songs unsurpassed among the folk songs of the world and, in the poignancy of their beauty, unequalled?" Johnson noted that when white America first heard the spirituals, they felt sympathy for the poor Negroes. By the 1920s he asserted that white Americans felt not pity but deference to the creative genius of the race. For Johnson this was yet another realization of black literature's power and its effect on race relations.

Because Johnson was able to bring white and black America together through his literary and other writings, I think of him as a linking agent for black America. He reduced and overcame many of the barriers that had made communication across the races so difficult, and that had long prevented the smooth and efficient transfer of knowledge. His ability to be an effective link was due to his deftness at blending two cultures in his literary works. For example, in *God's Trombones* he built on a premise that allowed him to fuse two traditions: He used the tradition of standard Bible English to express the developing black ethos. This fusion enabled him to establish a tradition that he called conscious art reared on the foundation of black folk art. He wrote, "When a Negro author does write so as to fuse white and black America into one interested and approving audience he has performed no slight feat, and has most likely done a sound piece of literary work." The noted philosopher Alain Locke maintained that Johnson's literary works were racial in substance but universal in appeal.

Further testament to Johnson's role as link between white and black America are his numerous essays published in white journals and newspapers, including *The Nation*, *Century*, *Harper's*, *The American Mercury*, *The New York Times*, and *The Herald Tribune*. Concurrently, his writings were appearing in black journals and newspapers, including *The Crisis*, *The New York Am-*

sterdam News, and *Opportunity*. In writing for two audiences, Johnson never missed an opportunity to do two things: interpret the cultural contributions of his race and extol black literature as an integral part of American literature. He consistently pointed out to both white and black Americans that "it is more or less generally acknowledged that the only things artistic that have sprung from American soil and out of American life, and been universally recognized as distinctively American products, are the folk creations of the Negro."

As New York University's first African-American professor, Johnson was the first of his race to teach African-American literature at a white university. Before Johnson died in 1938, Dean George Payne of New York University had worked with him to develop a special program that would have authorized Johnson to teach black literature at other universities across the nation on behalf of New York University. Thus, had he lived, African-American studies would have begun by the 1930s.

As a link, Johnson attempted to connect all Americans through literature by debunking the stereotypes about his people. Further, he used literature to call attention to the urgent political and social plight of black Americans. His novel, *The Autobiography of an Ex-Colored Man* (1912), relates the life of a character of mixed ancestry who passes for white. Addressing the subject of "passing" was not Johnson's true objective. Rather, he was addressing the social and political injustices that made "passing" a way out. He wanted to emphasize in this novel that, in America, the very fact that a person is black is adequate information to determine what should be thought of him and how he should be treated, that white America sees little need to find out who a black person is, or what his talents, interests, ambitions, and thoughts might be.[1]

In 1917 Johnson produced his first book of poetry, *Fifty Years and Other Poems*. This volume established him as the most cele-

[1]Paper on *The Autobiography of an Ex-Colored Man* by Charles S. Johnson, 1946. The James Weldon Johnson Collection, African-American Collections, Emory University, Atlanta, Georgia.

brated African-American poet since Paul Laurence Dunbar. Dun-
bar, who died in 1906, had written only in dialect, which was
wholly accepted by white Americans. But Johnson decided that
dialect was too narrow a medium to express the fullness of black
life. Dialect, Johnson wrote, "is an instrument with but two full
stops, humor and pathos." He further contended that the black
poet "needs a form that is freer and larger than dialect, but which
will still hold the racial flavor; a form expressing the imagery, the
idioms, the peculiar turns of thought, and which will be capable
of voicing the deepest and highest emotions and aspirations" of a
people. Johnson, in *Fifty Years and Other Poems*, presents poems
both in dialect and in traditional English, but which are racial in
substance. His friend and literary mentor, Columbia University's
Brander Matthews, describes this book as "a cry for recognition,
for sympathy, for understanding, and above all, for justice."

Johnson edited the first black anthology, *The Book of Ameri-
can Negro Poetry*, in 1922. This volume consists of a collection
of poems by African-American poets from 1750 to the 1920s. By
including such poets as Paul Laurence Dunbar, James David
Corrothers, Georgia Douglas Johnson, Countee Cullen, and Lang-
ston Hughes, Johnson reveals the undeniable creative genius of
black artists and their irrefutable contribution to American litera-
ture. In the noted preface to this volume, Johnson offered an ex-
planation for the work:

There is perhaps, a better excuse for giving an Anthology of
American Negro Poetry to the public than can be offered for
many of the anthologies that have recently been issued. The pub-
lic, generally speaking, does not know that there are American
Negro poets—to supply this lack of information is, alone, a
work worthy of somebody's effort. . . .

A people may become great through many means, but there is
only one measure by which its greatness is recognized and ac-
knowledged. The final measure of the greatness of all peoples is
the amount and standard of the literature and art they have pro-
duced. The world does not know that a people is great until that
people produces great literature and art. No people that has pro-
duced great literature and art has ever been looked upon by the
world as distinctly inferior.

The status of the Negro in the United States is more a question of national mental attitude toward the race than of actual conditions. And nothing will do more to change that mental attitude and raise his status than a demonstration of intellectual parity by the Negro through the production of literature and art.[2]

Johnson's third volume of poetry, *Saint Peter Relates an Incident* (1935), is a tribute to black patriotism as well as an indictment of racial inequities. These poems can be viewed within two contexts. The first consists of poems built upon racial themes but having some universal appeal—mainly protest poems and poems in dialect. The second is comprised of themes expressing entirely universal sentiments.

If I had to define the feelings, ideas, and thoughts of James Weldon Johnson as a litterateur and poet in one word, it would be *universality*. "Universality" because of his belief that it is through the production and interpretation of a race's literature and other creative expressions that a people can begin to break down the stereotypical conceptions that are so inherent in universal thought.

In his own literary canon, Johnson demonstrates that no one race can lay claim to universality. In "O Black and Unknown Bards," his prototypes of faceless and nameless slaves come to life as representatives of a universal human condition. In this poem and in much of his other literary writings, we see Johnson using the particular to explain the universal. And he concurrently uses the universal to explain the particular. "O Black and Unknown Bards" accentuates the unique creative genius of a people who, while enslaved, transformed their condition into the Negro spirituals. The slaves had brought forth such melodies as "Steal Away Jesus," "Go Down, Moses," and "In Dat Great Gettin' Up Mornin'." Johnson contended that the imagination of the "Black and Unknown Bards" was sparked by the vivid biblical stories they heard. They fused these stories with the suffering and pathos of their own lives in musical form. These creators didn't record

[2]*The Book of American Negro Poetry*, ed. James Weldon Johnson. New York: Harcourt Brace Jovanovich, 1969, p. 9.

their creations themselves, but Johnson became the instrument for reproducing the black racial spirit in literary art form.

His success as a poet is mainly anchored in the oral traditions of his people. He realized that it was only by relying on these sources—sometimes symbolic—that a people could withstand racism. The African-American tradition as conceived by Johnson was dependent on its ability to relate itself to the human situation of oppressed people in general and black people in particular. The extent that Johnson conveyed this empathy is the extent to which he can be said to be really successful.

Assuredly the African-American tradition in American litera-ture has its paternity more in James Weldon Johnson than in anyone else. As poet-writer Sterling Brown once said, "By his in-terpretations of Negro poetry and music, by occasional essays on the problems of Negro writers, and by his own creative work, James Weldon Johnson succeeded more than any predecessor in furthering the cause of Negro artists." Alain Locke postulated that "Mr. Johnson brought, indeed, the first intellectual sub-stance to the content of our poetry." In 1935 Johnson's NAACP successor, Walter White, wrote, "There is hardly a Negro artist who is not indebted to [Johnson] for spiritual and material assis-tance."

Although Johnson was a giant in sophisticated literary circles, he accomplished even more in the arena of civil rights. As leader of the NAACP during the 1920s, he sat at the center of black thought and action while giving direction and voice to the associ-ation's burgeoning movement of racial uplift. The fact that he could be a leader concurrently of the Harlem Renaissance and of the NAACP during the 1920s illustrates how closely the goals of the two movements conformed. It is this highly effective double role that distinguishes James Weldon Johnson as one of the ex-ceptional figures of the twentieth century.

The poetry presented here represents Johnson's faith in litera-ture as a means of diminishing racial prejudice. Moreover, much of his poetry underscores his inexorable faith in the founding principles of America while he extols a race in what he called "a work so glorious."

SUGGESTIONS FOR FURTHER READING

WORKS BY JAMES WELDON JOHNSON

Along This Way: The Autobiography of James Weldon Johnson. New York: Viking, 1933. Reprinted with an introduction by Sondra Kathryn Wilson, New York: Da Capo, 2000.

The Autobiography of an Ex-Colored Man. Boston: Sherman, French, 1912. Reprinted, New York: Penguin Classics, 1990. Reprinted with an introduction by Henry Louis Gates, Jr., New York: Alfred A. Knopf, 1990.

Black Manhattan. New York: Alfred A. Knopf, 1930. Reprinted with an introduction by Sondra Kathryn Wilson, New York: Da Capo, 1991.

The Book of American Negro Poetry. James Weldon Johnson, ed. New York: Harcourt Brace, 1922. Reprinted, New York: Harcourt Brace Jovanovich, 1969.

The Books of American Negro Spirituals. James Weldon Johnson and J. Rosamond Johnson, eds. New York: Viking, 1925. Reprinted, New York: Da Capo, 1989.

Fifty Years and Other Poems. Boston: Cornhill, 1917.

God's Trombones: Seven Negro Sermons in Verse. New York: Viking, 1927. Reprinted, New York: Penguin Classics, 1990. Produced on audio by Sondra Kathryn Wilson for Penguin-Highbridge, 1993.

Negro Americans, What Now? New York: Viking, 1934.

Saint Peter Relates an Incident: Selected Poems (also titled *Lift Every Voice and Sing*). New York: Viking, 1935. Reprinted with a preface by Sondra Kathryn Wilson, New York: Penguin Putnam, 2000.

The Second Book of American Negro Spirituals. James Weldon Johnson and J. Rosamond Johnson, eds. New York: Viking, 1926. Reprinted, New York: Da Capo, 1989.

SECONDARY SOURCES

Adelman, Lynn. "A Study of James Weldon Johnson." *Journal of Negro History* 52 (April 1967): 128–45.

Akar, John J. "An African View of Black Studies with International Dimensions." *CLA Journal* 14 (1970): 7–18.

Aptheker, Herbert. "Du Bois on James Weldon Johnson." *Journal of Negro History* 52 (April 1967): 224–27.

Bacote, Clarence A. "James Weldon Johnson and Atlanta University." *Phylon* 32 (Winter 1971): 333–43.

Baker, Houston. "A Forgotten Prototype: *The Autobiography of an Ex-Colored Man* and *Invisible Man*." In *Singers of Daybreak*, ed. by Houston Baker. Washington, D.C.: Howard University Press, 1974.

Barksdale, Howard Reed. "James Weldon Johnson as a Man of Letters." Master's thesis, Fisk University, 1936.

Bond, Julian, and Sondra Kathryn Wilson, eds. *Lift Every Voice and Sing: 100 Years, 100 Voices*. New York: Random House, 2000.

Bone, Robert. *The Negro Novel in America*. New Haven: Yale University Press, 1965.

Bontemps, Arna, ed. *The Harlem Renaissance Remembered*. New York: Dodd Mead, 1972.

Braithwaite, William Stanley. "A Review of the Autobiography of James Weldon Johnson." *Opportunity* 11 (1933): 376–78.

Bronz, Stephen H. *Roots of Negro Racial Consciousness, the 1920's: Three Harlem Renaissance Authors*. New York: Libra, 1964.

Canady, Nicholas. "*The Autobiography of an Ex-Colored Man* and the Traditions of Black Biography." *Obsidian* 6 (Spring–Summer 1980): 76–80.

Carroll, Richard A. "Black Racial Spirit: An Analysis of James Weldon Johnson's Critical Perspective." *Phylon* 32 (Winter 1971): 344–64.

Clark, Peter W. "A Study of the Poetry of James Weldon Johnson." Master's thesis, Xavier University, 1942.

Collier, Eugenia. "The Endless Journey of an Ex-Colored Man." *Phylon* 32 (Winter 1971): 365–73.

———. "James Weldon Johnson: Mirror of Change." *Phylon* 21 (Fourth Quarter, 1960): 351–59.

Copans, Sim J. "James Weldon Johnson et le patrimonie cultural des noirs africains." *Cahier de la compagnie Madeleine Renaud–Jean Louis Barrault* 61 (1967): 422–48.

Davis, Arthur P. *From the Dark Tower: Afro-American Writers 1900 to 1960*. Washington, D.C.: Howard University Press, 1974.

Fleming, Robert E. "Contemporary Themes in Johnson's *Autobiography of an Ex-Colored Man*." *Negro American Literature Forum* 4 (Winter 1970): 120–24, 141.

———. "Irony as a Key to Johnson's *The Autobiography of an Ex-Colored Man*." *American Literature* 43 (March 1971): 83–86.

Gates, Henry Louis, Jr. *Thirteen Ways of Looking at Black Men.* New York: Vintage, 1998.

———, Nellie Y. McKay, et al., eds. *The Norton Anthology of African American Literature.* New York: W. W. Norton, 1997.

Huggins, Nathan Irvin. *Harlem Renaissance.* New York: Oxford University Press, 1971.

Jackson, Miles, Jr. "James Weldon Johnson." *Black World* 19 (June 1970): 32–34.

———. "Literary History: Documentary Sidelights, James Weldon Johnson and Claude McKay." *Negro Digest* 17 (June 1968): 25–29.

Kostelanetz, Richard. "The Politics of Passing: The Fiction of James Weldon Johnson." *Negro American Literature Forum* 3 (March 1969): 22–24, 29.

Levy, Eugene. *James Weldon Johnson: Black Leader, Black Voice.* Chicago: University of Chicago Press, 1973.

———. "James Weldon Johnson." *In Black Leaders of the Twentieth Century,* John Hope Franklin and August Meier, eds. Chicago: University of Chicago Press, 1980.

Lewis, David Levering. *When Harlem Was in Vogue.* New York: Oxford University Press, 1989.

———, ed. *The Portable Harlem Renaissance Reader.* New York: Viking Penguin, 1994.

Logan, Rayford W., and Michael R. Winston, eds. *Dictionary of Negro Biography.* New York: W. W. Norton, 1981, pp. 353–57.

Long, Richard A. "A Weapon of My Song: The Poetry of James Weldon Johnson." *Phylon* 32 (Winter 1971): 374–82.

Mason, Julian. "James Weldon Johnson." In *Fifty Southern Writers After 1900.* Joseph M. Flora and Robert Bian, eds. New York: Greenwood, 1987, pp. 280–89.

Miller, Ruth, and Peter J. Katopes. "The Harlem Renaissance: Arna Bontemps, Countee Cullen, James Weldon Johnson, Claude McKay, and Jean Toomer." In *Black American Writers: Bibliographical Essays, Vol. 1, The Beginnings Through the Harlem Renaissance and Langston Hughes.* Thomas Inge, et al., eds. New York: St. Martin's, 1978, pp. 161–206.

Millican, Arthenia Bates. "James Weldon Johnson: In Quest of an Afrocentric Tradition for Black American Literature." Doctoral dissertation, Louisiana State University, 1972.

O'Sullivan, Maurice J. "Of Souls and Pottage: James Weldon Johnson's *The Autobiography of an Ex-Colored Man.*" *CLA Journal* 23 (September 1979): 60–70.

Ovington, Mary White. *The Walls Came Tumbling Down: The Autobiography of Mary White Ovington, a Founder of the NAACP.* New York: Schocken, 1947.

Price, Kenneth M., and Lawrence J. Oliver, eds. *Critical Essays on James Weldon Johnson.* New York: G. K. Hall, 1997.

Redding, J. Saunders. *To Make a Poet Black.* Chapel Hill: University of North Carolina Press, 1939. Reprinted, College Park, Md.: McGrath, 1968.

Rosenblatt, Roger. "*The Autobiography of an Ex-Colored Man* in Black Fiction." Cambridge, Mass.: Harvard University Press, 1974.

Sanquist, Eric J. *The Hammers of Creation: Folk Culture in Modern African-American Fiction.* Macon, Ga.: Mercer University Press, 1993.

Skerrett, Joseph T., Jr. "Irony and Symbolic Action in James Weldon Johnson's *The Autobiography of an Ex-Colored Man.*" *American Quarterly* 32 (Winter 1980): 540–48.

Starke, Catherine Juanita. *Black Portraiture in American Fiction: Stock Characters, Archetypes, and Individuals.* New York: Basic Books, 1971.

Whitlow, Roger. *Black American Literature: A Critical History.* Chicago: Nelson-Hall, 1973.

Wilson, Sondra Kathryn. "James Weldon Johnson." *Crisis*, Winter (January 1989): 48–51, 117, 118.

———, guest ed. "Collected Writings of James Weldon Johnson." *Langston Hughes Review* 7 (Spring/Fall 1989).

——— with Warren Marr. *Paying for Freedom: The Story of the NAACP Life Membership Program.* New York: NAACP Press, 1988.

———, ed. *The Selected Writings of James Weldon Johnson*, vols. 1 and 2. New York: Oxford University Press, 1995.

———, ed. *The Crisis Reader: Stories, Poems, and Essays from the NAACP's Crisis Magazine.* New York: Random House, 1999.

———, ed. *In Search of Democracy: The NAACP Writings of James Weldon Johnson, Walter White, and Roy Wilkins (1920–1977).* New York: Oxford University Press, 1999.

Wohlforth, Robert. "Dark Leader: James Weldon Johnson." *The New Yorker*, September 30, 1933, 20–24.

Young, James O. *Black Writers of the Thirties.* Baton Rouge: Louisiana State University Press, 1973.

COLLECTIONS

The James Weldon Johnson Papers in the James Weldon Johnson Memorial Collection of Negro Arts and Letters, Beinecke Library, Yale University, New Haven, Connecticut.

The James Weldon Johnson Papers in African-American Collections, Woodruff Library, Emory University, Atlanta, Georgia.

CHRONOLOGY

1871   Born to James and Helen Louise Dillet Johnson on June 17 in Jacksonville, Florida.

1884   Makes trip to New York City.

1886   Meets Frederick Douglass in Jacksonville.

1887   Graduates from Stanton School in Jacksonville. Enters Atlanta University Preparatory Division.

1890   Graduates from Atlanta University Preparatory Division. Enters Atlanta University's freshman class.

1891   Teaches school in Henry County, Georgia, during the summer following his freshman year.

1892   Atlanta University Oratory Prize for "The Best Methods of Removing the Disabilities of Caste from the Negro."

1893   Meets Paul Laurence Dunbar at the Chicago World's Fair.

1894   Receives B.A. degree with honors from Atlanta University. Delivers valedictory speech, "The Destiny of the Human Race." Tours New England with the Atlanta University Quartet for three months. Is appointed principal of Stanton School in Jacksonville, Florida, the largest African-American public school in the state.

1895   Founds the *Daily American*, an afternoon daily serving Jacksonville's black population.

1896   Expands Stanton School to high school status, making it the first public high school for blacks in the state of Florida.

1898   Becomes the first African American to be admitted to the Florida bar.

1900   Writes the lyrics to "Lift Every Voice and Sing" with music by his brother, J. Rosamond Johnson. Meets his future wife, Grace Elizabeth Nail, daughter of well-known Harlem businessman John Bennett Nail, in New York.

1901 Elected president of the Florida State Teachers Association. Nearly lynched in a Jacksonville park. This near lynching makes him realize that he cannot advance in the South.

1902 Resigns as principal of Stanton School. Moves to New York to form musical trio, Cole and the Johnson Brothers. As part of this trio he writes more than two hundred popular songs, many of which are used in Broadway productions.

1903 Attends graduate school at Columbia University, where he studies with Brander Matthews, professor of dramatic literature.

1904 Writes two songs for Theodore Roosevelt's presidential campaign. Becomes a member of the National Business League, an organization founded by Booker T. Washington. Receives honorary degree from Atlanta University. During this time he meets W. E. B. Du Bois, then professor at Atlanta University.

1905 Cole and the Johnson Brothers go on European tour. Becomes president of Colored Republican Club in New York City.

1906 Accepts membership in the American Society of International Law. Is appointed U.S. consul to Venezuela by President Theodore Roosevelt.

1909 Is promoted to U.S. consul to Corinto, Nicaragua.

1910 Marries Grace Nail on February 3, in New York City.

1912 Publishes anonymously *The Autobiography of an Ex-Colored Man*, one of the earliest first-person narratives in fiction written by an African American.

1913 Resigns from the consular service on account of race prejudice and party politics.

1914 Accepts position at *The New York Age* as contributing editor. Becomes a founding member of the American

Society of Composers, Authors and Publishers (ASCAP).
Joins Sigma Pi Phi fraternity and Phi Beta Sigma
fraternity.

1915   Becomes member of the NAACP. Puts into English the
libretto of *Goyescas*, the Spanish grand opera, which is
produced at the Metropolitan Opera House.

1916   Attends the NAACP conference in Amenia, New York,
at the estate of J. E. Spingarn. Delivers speech "A Work-
ing Programme for the Future." Joins the staff of the
NAACP in the position of field secretary.

1917   Publishes volume *Fifty Years and Other Poems*.
Publishes poem "Saint Peter Relates an Incident of the
Resurrection Day." With W. E. B. Du Bois, leads over
12,000 marchers down New York's Fifth Avenue to
protest lynchings and riots. Becomes acting secretary of
the NAACP. Supports U.S. entry into World War I and
fights against the atrocities perpetrated against black
soldiers. Meets Walter White in Atlanta and persuades
him to join the staff of the NAACP. Attends conference
of the Intercollegiate Socialist Society in Bellport, New
York; gives talk on the contribution of the Negro to
American culture. With W. E. B. Du Bois becomes
charter member of the Civic Club, a liberal club that
grows to be a strong influence in the life of black New
Yorkers.

1918   Is responsible for an unprecedented increase in NAACP
membership in one year, particularly in the South,
making the NAACP a national power.

1919   Participates in converting the National Civil Liberties
Bureau into a permament organization, the American
Civil Liberties Union.

1920   NAACP board of directors names him secretary (chief
executive officer), making him the first African
American to serve in that position. Based on his earlier
investigation of the American occupation of Haiti, he
publishes four articles, titled "Self-Determining Haiti."

1922 Publishes *The Book of American Negro Poetry*.

1924 Assists several writers of the Harlem Renaissance.

1925 Receives NAACP's Spingarn Medal. Co-authors with J. Rosamond Johnson *The Book of American Negro Spirituals*.

1926 Co-authors with J. Rosamond Johnson *The Second Book of American Negro Spirituals*. Purchases an old farm in the Massachusetts Berkshires and builds a summer cottage called "Five Acres."

1927 During the height of the Harlem Renaissance, *The Autobiography of an Ex-Coloured Man* is reprinted. (The spelling *coloured* was used to attract British sales of the book.) *God's Trombones* is published.

1928 Receives Harmon Award for *God's Trombones*. Receives D.Litt. from Howard University and Talledega College.

1929 Takes a leave of absence from the NAACP. Attends the Third Japanese Biennial Conference on Pacific Relations. Receives Julius Rosenwald Fellowship to write *Black Manhattan*.

1930 *Black Manhattan*, a history of African Americans in New York City from the seventeenth century to the 1920s, is published.

1931 Publishes the revised and enlarged edition of *The Book of American Negro Poetry*. NAACP honors him by hosting a testimonial dinner in New York City attended by more than three hundred guests. Is appointed vice president and board member of the NAACP. Accepts Fisk University appointment as the Adam K. Spence Professor of Creative Literature.

1933 Publishes autobiography *Along This Way*. Attends the second NAACP Amenia Conference.

1934 Is appointed visiting professor, fall semester, at New York University, becoming the first African American to hold such a position at the institution. Receives the

Du Bois Prize for *Black Manhattan* as the best book of prose written by an African American during a three-year period. Publishes *Negro Americans, What Now?*

1935   Publishes *Saint Peter Relates an Incident: Selected Poems*.

1938   Dies as a result of an automobile accident in Wiscassett, Maine, on June 26, nine days after his sixty-seventh birthday. Funeral held at the Salem Methodist Church in Harlem on Thursday, June 30. Is cremated.*

*Mrs. James Weldon Johnson (Grace Nail Johnson) died on November 1, 1976. Grace and James Weldon Johnson were interred together by Ollie Jewel Sims Okala on November 19, 1976, in the Nail family plot in Green-Wood Cemetery in Brooklyn, New York.

JAMES WELDON JOHNSON

COMPLETE POEMS

PART I

God's Trombones:
Seven Negro Sermons in Verse

JAMES WELDON JOHNSON's search for an African-American tradition in American literature was initially unintentional. Born into a sedate family steeped in European values, he ultimately stumbled upon another world replete with "black mass" values. It was this discovery that led him to the hidden treasure of black folk art.

The revelation that brought about his transformation regarding black poetry came by way of an old-time Kansas City preacher. This sermonizer inspired Johnson's poem "The Creation," which was first published in 1918. Johnson writes about the preacher's influence upon him, "The preacher strode the pulpit up and down in what was actually a rhythmic dance and he brought into play a full gamut of his wonderful voice which excited my envy. He intoned, he moaned, he pleaded—he blared, he crashed, he thundered." Deeply moved, Johnson took out a slip of paper and began writing the poem "The Creation." This poem, extracted from the oral folk tradition, represents the documentation of a people's culture. In 1927 Johnson published "The Creation" with six other poems under the title God's Trombones: Seven Negro Sermons in Verse. In this volume he transformed the old-time preachers' orations into original and moving poetry, and in doing so, ensured the survival of a people's great oral tradition.

Preface

A GOOD DEAL has been written on the folk creations of the American Negro: his music, sacred and secular; his plantation tales, and his dances; but that there are folk sermons, as well, is a fact that has passed unnoticed. I remember hearing in my boyhood sermons that were current, sermons that passed with only slight modifications from preacher to preacher and from locality to locality. Such sermons were, "The Valley of Dry Bones," which was based on the vision of the prophet in the 37th chapter of Ezekiel; the "Train Sermon," in which both God and the devil were pictured as running trains, one loaded with saints, that pulled up in heaven, and the other with sinners, that dumped its load in hell; the "Heavenly March," which gave in detail the journey of the faithful from earth, on up through the pearly gates to the great white throne. Then there was a stereotyped sermon which had no definite subject, and which was quite generally preached; it began with the Creation, went on to the fall of man, rambled through the trials and tribulations of the Hebrew Children, came down to the redemption by Christ, and ended with the Judgment Day and a warning and an exhortation to sinners. This was the framework of a sermon that allowed the individual preacher the widest latitude that could be desired for all his arts and powers. There was one Negro sermon that in its day was a classic, and widely known to the public. Thousands of people, white and black, flocked to the church of John Jasper in Richmond, Virginia, to hear him preach his famous sermon proving that the earth is flat and the sun does move. John Jasper's sermon was imitated and adapted by many lesser preachers.

I heard only a few months ago in Harlem an up-to-date version of the "Train Sermon." The preacher styled himself "Son of Thunder"—a sobriquet adopted by many of the old-time preachers—and phrased his subject, "The Black Diamond Express, running between here and hell, making thirteen stops and arriving in hell ahead of time."

The old-time Negro preacher has not yet been given the niche in which he properly belongs. He has been portrayed only as a semi-comic figure. He had, it is true, his comic aspects, but on the whole he was an important figure, and at bottom a vital factor. It was through him that the people of diverse languages and customs who were brought here from diverse parts of Africa and thrown into slavery were given their first sense of unity and solidarity. He was the first shepherd of this bewildered flock. His power for good or ill was very great. It was the old-time preacher who for generations was the mainspring of hope and inspiration for the Negro in America. It was also he who instilled into the Negro the narcotic doctrine epitomized in the Spiritual, "You May Have All Dis World, But Give Me Jesus." This power of the old-time preacher, somewhat lessened and changed in his successors, is still a vital force; in fact, it is still the greatest single influence among the colored people of the United States. The Negro today is, perhaps, the most priest-governed group in the country.

The history of the Negro preacher reaches back to Colonial days. Before the Revolutionary War, when slavery had not yet taken on its more grim and heartless economic aspects, there were famed black preachers who preached to both whites and blacks. George Liele was preaching to whites and blacks at Augusta, Ga., as far back as 1773, and Andrew Bryan at Savannah a few years later.* The most famous of these earliest preachers was Black Harry, who during the Revolutionary period accompanied Bishop Asbury as a drawing card and preached from the same platform with other founders of the Methodist Church. Of him, John Ledman in his *History of the Rise of Methodism in America* says, "The truth was that Harry was a more popular speaker than Mr. Asbury or almost anyone else in his day." In the two or three decades before the Civil War Negro preachers in the North, many of them well-educated and cultured, were courageous spokesmen against slavery and all its evils.

The effect on the Negro of the establishment of separate and independent places of worship can hardly be estimated. Some idea of how far this effect reached may be gained by a compari-

*See *The History of the Negro Church*, Carter G. Woodson.

son between the social and religious trends of the Negroes of the Old South and of the Negroes of French Louisiana and the West Indies, where they were within and directly under the Roman Catholic Church and the Church of England. The old-time preacher brought about the establishment of these independent places of worship and thereby provided the first sphere in which race leadership might develop and function. These scattered and often clandestine groups have grown into the strongest and richest organization among colored Americans. Another thought—except for these separate places of worship there never would have been any Spirituals.

The old-time preacher was generally a man far above the average in intelligence; he was, not infrequently, a man of positive genius. The earliest of these preachers must have virtually committed many parts of the Bible to memory through hearing the scriptures read or preached from in the white churches which the slaves attended. They were the first of the slaves to learn to read, and their reading was confined to the Bible, and specifically to the more dramatic passages of the Old Testament. A text served mainly as a starting point and often had no relation to the development of the sermon. Nor would the old-time preacher balk at any text within the lids of the Bible. There is the story of one who after reading a rather cryptic passage took off his spectacles, closed the Bible with a bang and by way of preface said, "Brothers and sisters, this morning—I intend to explain the unexplainable—find out the undefinable—ponder over the imponderable—and unscrew the inscrutable."

* * *

The old-time Negro preacher of parts was above all an orator, and in good measure an actor. He knew the secret of oratory, that at bottom it is a progression of rhythmic words more than it is anything else. Indeed, I have witnessed congregations moved to ecstasy by the rhythmic intoning of sheer incoherencies. He was a master of all the modes of eloquence. He often possessed a voice that was a marvelous instrument, a voice he could modulate from a sepulchral whisper to a crashing thunder clap. His discourse was generally kept at a high pitch of fervency, but occasionally he dropped into colloquialisms and, less often, into humor. He preached a personal and anthropomorphic God, a sure-enough heaven and a red-hot hell. His imagination was bold and unfettered. He had the power to sweep his hearers before him; and so himself was often swept away. At such times his language was not prose but poetry. It was from memories of such preachers there grew the idea of this book of poems.

* * *

In a general way, these poems were suggested by the rather vague memories of sermons I heard preached in my childhood; but the immediate stimulus for setting them down came quite definitely at a comparatively recent date. I was speaking on a Sunday in Kansas City, addressing meetings in various colored churches. When I had finished my fourth talk it was after nine o'clock at night, but the committee told me there was still another meeting to address. I demurred, making the quotation about the willingness of the spirit and the weakness of the flesh, for I was dead tired. I also protested the lateness of the hour, but I was informed that for the meeting at this church we were in good time. When we reached the church an "exhorter" was just concluding a dull sermon. After his there were two other short sermons. These sermons proved to be preliminaries, mere curtain-raisers for a famed visiting preacher. At last he arose. He was a dark-brown man, handsome in his gigantic proportions. He appeared to be a bit self-conscious, perhaps impressed by the presence of the "distinguished visitor" on the platform, and started in to preach a formal sermon from a formal text. The congregation sat apathetic and dozing. He sensed that he was losing his audience and his opportunity. Suddenly he closed the Bible, stepped out from behind the pulpit and began to preach. He started intoning the old folk-sermon that begins with the creation of the world and ends with Judgment Day. He was at once a changed man, free, at ease and masterful. The change in the congregation was instantaneous. An electric current ran through the crowd. It was in a moment alive and quivering; and all the while the preacher held it in the palm of his hand. He was wonderful in the way he employed his conscious and unconscious art. He strode the pulpit up and down in what was actually a very rhythmic dance, and he brought into play the full gamut of his wonderful voice, a voice—what shall I say?—not of an organ or a trumpet, but rather of a trombone,* the instrument possessing above all others the power to express the wide and varied range of emotions encompassed by the human voice—and with greater amplitude. He intoned, he moaned, he pleaded—he blared, he crashed, he thundered. I sat fascinated; and more, I was, perhaps against my will, deeply moved; the emotional effect upon me was irresistible. Before he had finished I took a slip of paper and somewhat surreptitiously jotted down some ideas for the first poem, "The Creation."

* * *

At first thought, Negro dialect would appear to be the precise medium for these old-time sermons; however, as the reader will see, the poems are not written in dialect. My reason for not using the dialect is double. First, although the dialect is the exact instrument for voicing certain traditional phases of Negro life, it is, and perhaps by that very exactness, a quite limited instrument. Indeed, it is an instrument with but two complete stops, pathos and humor. This limitation is not due to any defect of the dialect as dialect, but to the mould of convention in which Negro dialect in the United States has been set, to the fixing effects of its long association with the Negro only as a happy-go-lucky or a forlorn figure. The Aframerican poet might in time be able to break this mould of convention and write poetry in dialect without feeling that his first line will put the reader in a frame of mind which demands that the poem be either funny or sad, but I doubt that he will make the effort to do it; he does not consider it worth the while. In fact, practically no poetry is being written in dialect by the colored poets of today. These poets have thrown aside dialect and discarded most of the material and subject matter that went into dialect poetry. The passing of dialect as a medium for Negro poetry will be an actual loss, for in it many beautiful things can be done, and done best; however, in my opinion, *traditional* Negro dialect as a form for Aframerican poets is absolutely dead.

Trombone: A powerful brass instrument of the trumpet family, the only wind instrument possessing a complete chromatic scale enharmonically true, like the human voice or the violin, and hence very valuable in the orchestra.—*Standard Dictionary.*

The Negro poet in the United States, for poetry which he wishes to give a distinctively racial tone and color, needs now an instrument of greater range than dialect; that is, if he is to do more than sound the small notes of sentimentality. I said something on this point in *The Book of American Negro Poetry*, and because I cannot say it better, I quote: "What the colored poet in the United States needs to do is something like what Synge did for the Irish; he needs to find a form that will express the racial spirit by symbols from within rather than by symbols from without—such as the mere mutilation of English spelling and pronunciation. He needs a form that is freer and larger than dialect, but which will still hold the racial flavor; a form expressing the imagery, the idioms, the peculiar turns of thought and the distinctive humor and pathos, too, of the Negro, but which will also be capable of voicing the deepest and highest emotions and aspirations and allow of the widest range of subjects and the widest scope of treatment." The form of "The Creation," the first poem of this group, was a first experiment by me in this direction.

The second part of my reason for not writing these poems in dialect is the weightier. The old-time Negro preachers, though they actually used dialect in their ordinary intercourse, stepped out from its narrow confines when they preached. They were all saturated with the sublime phraseology of the Hebrew prophets and steeped in the idioms of King James English, so when they preached and warmed to their work they spoke another language, a language far removed from traditional Negro dialect. It was really a fusion of Negro idioms with Bible English; and in this there may have been, after all, some kinship with the innate grandiloquence of their old African tongues. To place in the mouths of the talented old-time Negro preachers a language that is a literary imitation of Mississippi cotton-field dialect is sheer burlesque.

Gross exaggeration of the use of big words by these preachers, in fact by Negroes in general, has been commonly made; the laugh being at the exhibition of ignorance involved. What is the basis of this fondness for big words? Is the predilection due, as is supposed, to ignorance desiring to parade itself as knowledge? Not at all. The old-time Negro preacher loved the sonorous, mouth-filling, ear-filling phrase because it gratified a highly developed sense of sound and rhythm in himself and his hearers.

* * *

I claim no more for these poems than that I have written them after the manner of the primitive sermons. In the writing of them I have, naturally, felt the influence of the Spirituals. There is, of course, no way of recreating the atmosphere—the fervor of the congregation, the amens and hallelujahs, the undertone of singing which was often a soft accompaniment to parts of the sermon; nor the personality of the preacher—his physical magnetism, his gestures and gesticulations, his changes of tempo, his pauses for effect, and, more than all, his tones of voice. These poems would better be intoned than read; especially does this apply to "Listen, Lord," "The Crucifixion," and "The Judgment Day." But the intoning practiced by the old-time preacher is a thing next to impossible to describe; it must be heard, and it is extremely difficult to imitate even when heard. The finest, and perhaps the only demonstration ever given to a New York public, was the intoning of the dream in Ridgely Torrence's *Rider of Dreams* by Opal Cooper of the Negro Players at the Madison Square Theatre in 1917. Those who were fortunate enough to hear him can never, I know, forget the thrill of it. This intoning is always a matter of crescendo and diminuendo in the intensity—a rising and falling between plain speaking and wild chanting. And often a startling effect is gained by breaking off suddenly at the highest point of intensity and dropping into the monotone of ordinary speech.

The tempos of the preacher I have endeavored to indicate by the line arrangement of the poems, and a certain sort of pause that is marked by a quick intaking and an audible expulsion of the breath I have indicated by dashes. There is a decided syncopation of speech—the crowding in of many syllables or the lengthening out of a few to fill one metrical foot, the sensing of which must be left to the reader's ear. The rhythmical stress of this syncopation is partly obtained by a marked silent fraction of a beat; frequently this silent fraction is filled in by a hand clap.

One factor in the creation of atmosphere I have included—the preliminary prayer. The prayer leader was sometimes a woman. It was the prayer leader who directly prepared the way for the sermon, set the scene, as it were. However, a most impressive concomitant of the prayer, the chorus of responses which gave it an antiphonal quality, I have not attempted to set down. These preliminary prayers were often products hardly less remarkable than the sermons.

* * *

The old-time Negro preacher is rapidly passing. I have here tried sincerely to fix something of him.

New York City, 1927.

Listen, Lord—A Prayer

O Lord, we come this morning
Knee-bowed and body-bent
Before thy throne of grace.
O Lord—this morning—
Bow our hearts beneath our knees,
And our knees in some lonesome valley.
We come this morning—
Like empty pitchers to a full fountain,
With no merits of our own.
O Lord—open up a window of heaven,
And lean out far over the battlements of glory,
And listen this morning.

Lord, have mercy on proud and dying sinners—
Sinners hanging over the mouth of hell,
Who seem to love their distance well.
Lord—ride by this morning—
Mount your milk-white horse,
And ride-a this morning—
And in your ride, ride by old hell,
Ride by the dingy gates of hell,
And stop poor sinners in their headlong plunge.

And now, O Lord, this man of God,
Who breaks the bread of life this morning—
Shadow him in the hollow of thy hand,
And keep him out of the gunshot of the devil.
Take him, Lord—this morning—
Wash him with hyssop inside and out,
Hang him up and drain him dry of sin.
Pin his ear to the wisdom-post,
And make his words sledge hammers of truth—
Beating on the iron heart of sin.
Lord God, this morning—
Put his eye to the telescope of eternity,

And let him look upon the paper walls of time.
Lord, turpentine his imagination,
Put perpetual motion in his arms,
Fill him full of the dynamite of thy power,
Anoint him all over with the oil of thy salvation,
And set his tongue on fire.

And now, O Lord—
When I've done drunk my last cup of sorrow—
When I've been called everything but a child of God—
When I'm done travelling up the rough side of the mountain—
O—Mary's Baby—
When I start down the steep and slippery steps of death—
When this old world begins to rock beneath my feet—
Lower me to my dusty grave in peace
To wait for that great gittin' up morning—Amen.

The Creation

And God stepped out on space,
And he looked around and said:
I'm lonely—
I'll make me a world.

And far as the eye of God could see
Darkness covered everything,
Blacker than a hundred midnights
Down in a cypress swamp.

Then God smiled,
And the light broke,
And the darkness rolled up on one side,
And the light stood shining on the other,
And God said: That's good!

Then God reached out and took the light in his hands,
And God rolled the light around in his hands
Until he made the sun;
And he set that sun a-blazing in the heavens.
And the light that was left from making the sun
God gathered it up in a shining ball
And flung it against the darkness,
Spangling the night with the moon and stars.
Then down between
The darkness and the light
He hurled the world;
And God said: That's good!

Then God himself stepped down—
And the sun was on his right hand,
And the moon was on his left;
The stars were clustered about his head,
And the earth was under his feet.
And God walked, and where he trod

His footsteps hollowed the valleys out
And bulged the mountains up.

Then he stopped and looked and saw
That the earth was hot and barren.
So God stepped over to the edge of the world
And he spat out the seven seas—
He batted his eyes, and the lightnings flashed—
He clapped his hands, and the thunders rolled—
And the waters above the earth came down,
The cooling waters came down.

Then the green grass sprouted,
And the little red flowers blossomed,
The pine tree pointed his finger to the sky,
And the oak spread out his arms,
The lakes cuddled down in the hollows of the ground,
And the rivers ran down to the sea;
And God smiled again,
And the rainbow appeared,
And curled itself around his shoulder.

Then God raised his arm and he waved his hand
Over the sea and over the land,
And he said: Bring forth! Bring forth!
And quicker than God could drop his hand,
Fishes and fowls
And beasts and birds
Swam the rivers and the seas,
Roamed the forests and the woods,
And split the air with their wings.
And God said: That's good!

Then God walked around,
And God looked around
On all that he had made.
He looked at his sun,
And he looked at his moon,

And he looked at his little stars;
He looked on his world
With all its living things,
And God said: I'm lonely still.

Then God sat down—
On the side of a hill where he could think;
By a deep, wide river he sat down;
With his head in his hands,
God thought and thought,
Till he thought: I'll make me a man!

Up from the bed of the river
God scooped the clay;
And by the bank of the river
He kneeled him down;
And there the great God Almighty
Who lit the sun and fixed it in the sky,
Who flung the stars to the most far corner of the night,
Who rounded the earth in the middle of his hand;
This Great God,
Like a mammy bending over her baby,
Kneeled down in the dust
Toiling over a lump of clay
Till he shaped it in his own image;

Then into it he blew the breath of life,
And man became a living soul.
Amen.   Amen.

The Prodigal Son

Young man—
Young man—
Your arm's too short to box with God.

But Jesus spake in a parable, and he said:
A certain man had two sons.
Jesus didn't give this man a name,
But his name is God Almighty.
And Jesus didn't call these sons by name,
But ev'ry young man,
Ev'rywhere,
Is one of these two sons.

And the younger son said to his father,
He said: Father, divide up the property,
And give me my portion now.

And the father with tears in his eyes said: Son,
Don't leave your father's house.
But the boy was stubborn in his head,
And haughty in his heart,
And he took his share of his father's goods,
And went into a far-off country.

There comes a time,
There comes a time
When ev'ry young man looks out from his father's house,
Longing for that far-off country.

And the young man journeyed on his way,
And he said to himself as he travelled along:
This sure is an easy road,
Nothing like the rough furrows behind my father's plow.

Young man—
Young man—
Smooth and easy is the road
That leads to hell and destruction.
Down grade all the way,
The further you travel, the faster you go.
No need to trudge and sweat and toil,
Just slip and slide and slip and slide
Till you bang up against hell's iron gate.

And the younger son kept travelling along,
Till at night-time he came to a city.
And the city was bright in the night-time like day,
The streets all crowded with people,
Brass bands and string bands a-playing,
And ev'rywhere the young man turned
There was singing and laughing and dancing.
And he stopped a passer-by and he said:
Tell me what city is this?
And the passer-by laughed and said: Don't you know?
This is Babylon, Babylon,
That great city of Babylon.
Come on, my friend, and go along with me.
And the young man joined the crowd.

Young man—
Young man—
You're never lonesome in Babylon.
You can always join a crowd in Babylon.
Young man—
Young man—
You can never be alone in Babylon,
Alone with your Jesus in Babylon.
You can never find a place, a lonesome place,
A lonesome place to go down on your knees,
And talk with your God, in Babylon.
You're always in a crowd in Babylon.

And the young man went with his new-found friend,
And bought himself some brand new clothes,
And he spent his days in the drinking dens,
Swallowing the fires of hell.
And he spent his nights in the gambling dens,
Throwing dice with the devil for his soul.
And he met up with the women of Babylon.
Oh, the women of Babylon!
Dressed in yellow and purple and scarlet,
Loaded with rings and earrings and bracelets,
Their lips like a honeycomb dripping with honey,
Perfumed and sweet-smelling like a jasmine flower;
And the jasmine smell of the Babylon women
Got in his nostrils and went to his head,
And he wasted his substance in riotous living,
In the evening, in the black and dark of night,
With the sweet-sinning women of Babylon.
And they stripped him of his money,
And they stripped him of his clothes,
And they left him broke and ragged
In the streets of Babylon.

Then the young man joined another crowd—
The beggars and lepers of Babylon.
And he went to feeding swine,
And he was hungrier than the hogs;
He got down on his belly in the mire and mud
And ate the husks with the hogs.
And not a hog was too low to turn up his nose
At the man in the mire of Babylon.

Then the young man came to himself—
He came to himself and said:
In my father's house are many mansions,
Ev'ry servant in his house has bread to eat,
Ev'ry servant in his house has a place to sleep;
I will arise and go to my father.

And his father saw him afar off,
And he ran up the road to meet him.
He put clean clothes upon his back,
And a golden chain around his neck,
He made a feast and killed the fatted calf,
And invited the neighbors in.

Oh-o-oh, sinner,
When you're mingling with the crowd in Babylon—
Drinking the wine of Babylon—
Running with the women of Babylon—
You forget about God, and you laugh at Death.
Today you've got the strength of a bull in your neck
And the strength of a bear in your arms,
But some o' these days, some o' these days,
You'll have a hand-to-hand struggle with bony Death,
And Death is bound to win.

Young man, come away from Babylon,
That hell-border city of Babylon.
Leave the dancing and gambling of Babylon,
The wine and whiskey of Babylon,
The hot-mouthed women of Babylon;
Fall down on your knees,
And say in your heart:
I will arise and go to my Father.

Go Down Death—A Funeral Sermon

Weep not, weep not,
She is not dead;
She's resting in the bosom of Jesus.
Heart-broken husband—weep no more;
Grief-stricken son—weep no more;
Left-lonesome daughter—weep no more;
She's only just gone home.

Day before yesterday morning,
God was looking down from his great, high heaven,
Looking down on all his children,
And his eye fell on Sister Caroline,
Tossing on her bed of pain.
And God's big heart was touched with pity,
With the everlasting pity.

And God sat back on his throne,
And he commanded that tall, bright angel standing at his right hand:
Call me Death!
And that tall, bright angel cried in a voice
That broke like a clap of thunder:
Call Death!—Call Death!
And the echo sounded down the streets of heaven
Till it reached away back to that shadowy place,
Where Death waits with his pale, white horses.

And Death heard the summons,
And he leaped on his fastest horse,
Pale as a sheet in the moonlight.
Up the golden street Death galloped,
And the hoofs of his horse struck fire from the gold,
But they didn't make no sound.
Up Death rode to the Great White Throne,
And waited for God's command.

And God said: Go down, Death, go down,
Go down to Savannah, Georgia,
Down in Yamacraw,
And find Sister Caroline.
She's borne the burden and heat of the day,
She's labored long in my vineyard,
And she's tired—
She's weary—
Go down, Death, and bring her to me.

And Death didn't say a word,
But he loosed the reins on his pale, white horse,
And he clamped the spurs to his bloodless sides,
And out and down he rode,
Through heaven's pearly gates,
Past suns and moons and stars;
On Death rode,
And the foam from his horse was like a comet in the sky;
On Death rode,
Leaving the lightning's flash behind;
Straight on down he came.

While we were watching round her bed,
She turned her eyes and looked away,
She saw what we couldn't see;
She saw Old Death. She saw Old Death
Coming like a falling star.
But Death didn't frighten Sister Caroline;
He looked to her like a welcome friend.
And she whispered to us: I'm going home,
And she smiled and closed her eyes.

And Death took her up like a baby,
And she lay in his icy arms,
But she didn't feel no chill.
And Death began to ride again—
Up beyond the evening star,
Out beyond the morning star,

Into the glittering light of glory,
On to the Great White Throne.
And there he laid Sister Caroline
On the loving breast of Jesus.

And Jesus took his own hand and wiped away her tears,
And he smoothed the furrows from her face,
And the angels sang a little song,
And Jesus rocked her in his arms,
And kept a-saying: Take your rest,
Take your rest, take your rest.

Weep not—weep not,
She is not dead;
She's resting in the bosom of Jesus.

Noah Built the Ark

In the cool of the day—
God was walking—
Around in the Garden of Eden.
And except for the beasts, eating in the fields,
And except for the birds, flying through the trees,
The garden looked like it was deserted.
And God called out and said: Adam,
Adam, where art thou?
And Adam, with Eve behind his back,
Came out from where he was hiding.

And God said: Adam,
What hast thou done?
Thou hast eaten of the tree!
And Adam,
With his head hung down,
Blamed it on the woman.

For after God made the first man Adam,
He breathed a sleep upon him;
Then he took out of Adam one of his ribs,
And out of that rib made woman.
And God put the man and woman together
In the beautiful Garden of Eden,
With nothing to do the whole day long
But play all around in the garden.
And God called Adam before him,
And he said to him:
Listen now, Adam,
Of all the fruit in the garden you can eat,
Except of the tree of knowledge;
For the day thou eatest of that tree,
Thou shalt surely die.

Then pretty soon along came Satan.
Old Satan came like a snake in the grass
To try out his tricks on the woman.
I imagine I can see Old Satan now
A-sidling up to the woman.
I imagine the first word Satan said was:
Eve, you're surely good looking.
I imagine he brought her a present, too,—
And, if there was such a thing in those ancient days,
He brought her a looking-glass.

And Eve and Satan got friendly—
Then Eve got to walking on shaky ground;
Don't ever get friendly with Satan.—
And they started to talk about the garden,
And Satan said: Tell me, how do you like
The fruit on the nice, tall, blooming tree
Standing in the middle of the garden?
And Eve said:
That's the forbidden fruit,
Which if we eat we die.

And Satan laughed a devilish little laugh,
And he said to the woman: God's fooling you, Eve;
That's the sweetest fruit in the garden.
I know you can eat that forbidden fruit,
And I know that you will not die.

And Eve looked at the forbidden fruit,
And it was red and ripe and juicy.
And Eve took a taste, and she offered it to Adam,
And Adam wasn't able to refuse;
So he took a bite, and they both sat down
And ate the forbidden fruit.—
Back there, six thousand years ago,
Man first fell by woman—
Lord, and he's doing the same today.

And that's how sin got into this world.
And man, as he multiplied on the earth,
Increased in wickedness and sin.
He went on down from sin to sin,
From wickedness to wickedness,
Murder and lust and violence,
All kinds of fornications,
Till the earth was corrupt and rotten with flesh,
An abomination in God's sight.

And God was angry at the sins of men.
And God got sorry that he ever made man.
And he said: I will destroy him.
I'll bring down judgment on him with a flood.
I'll destroy ev'rything on the face of the earth,
Man, beasts and birds, and creeping things.
And he did—
Ev'rything but the fishes.

But Noah was a just and righteous man.
Noah walked and talked with God.
And, one day, God said to Noah,
He said: Noah, build thee an ark.
Build it out of gopher wood.
Build it good and strong.
Pitch it within and pitch it without.
And build it according to the measurements
That I will give to thee.
Build it for you and all your house,
And to save the seeds of life on earth;
For I'm going to send down a mighty flood
To destroy this wicked world.

And Noah commenced to work on the ark.
And he worked for about one hundred years.
And ev'ry day the crowd came round
To make fun of Old Man Noah.

And they laughed and they said: Tell us, old man,
Where do you expect to sail that boat
Up here amongst the hills?

But Noah kept on a-working.
And ev'ry once in a while Old Noah would stop,
He'd lay down his hammer and lay down his saw,
And take his staff in hand;
And with his long, white beard a-flying in the wind,
And the gospel light a-gleaming from his eye,
Old Noah would preach God's word:

Sinners, oh, sinners,
Repent, for the judgment is at hand.
Sinners, oh, sinners,
Repent, for the time is drawing nigh.
God's wrath is gathering in the sky.
God's a-going to rain down rain on rain.
God's a-going to loosen up the bottom of the deep,
And drown this wicked world.
Sinners, repent while yet there's time
For God to change his mind.

Some smart young fellow said: This old man's
Got water on the brain.
And the crowd all laughed—Lord, but didn't they laugh;
And they paid no mind to Noah,
But kept on sinning just the same.

One bright and sunny morning,
Not a cloud nowhere to be seen,
God said to Noah: Get in the ark!
And Noah and his folks all got in the ark,
And all the animals, two by two,
A he and a she marched in.
Then God said: Noah, Bar the door!
And Noah barred the door.

And a little black spot begun to spread,
Like a bottle of ink spilling over the sky;
And the thunder rolled like a rumbling drum;
And the lightning jumped from pole to pole;
And it rained down rain, rain, rain,
Great God, but didn't it rain!
For forty days and forty nights
Waters poured down and waters gushed up;
And the dry land turned to sea.
And the old ark-a she begun to ride;
The old ark-a she begun to rock;
Sinners came a-running down to the ark;
Sinners came a-swimming all round the ark;
Sinners pleaded and sinners prayed—
Sinners wept and sinners wailed—
But Noah'd done barred the door.

And the trees and the hills and the mountain tops
Slipped underneath the waters.
And the old ark sailed that lonely sea—
For twelve long months she sailed that sea,
A sea without a shore.

Then the waters begun to settle down,
And the ark touched bottom on the tallest peak
Of old Mount Ararat.
The dove brought Noah the olive leaf,
And Noah when he saw that the grass was green,
Opened up the ark, and they all climbed down,
The folks, and the animals, two by two,
Down from the mount to the valley.
And Noah wept and fell on his face
And hugged and kissed the dry ground.

And then—

God hung out his rainbow cross the sky,
And he said to Noah: That's my sign!
No more will I judge the world by flood—
Next time I'll rain down fire.

The Crucifixion

Jesus, my gentle Jesus,
Walking in the dark of the Garden—
The Garden of Gethsemane,
Saying to the three disciples:
Sorrow is in my soul—
Even unto death;
Tarry ye here a little while,
And watch with me.

Jesus, my burdened Jesus,
Praying in the dark of the Garden—
The Garden of Gethsemane.
Saying: Father,
Oh, Father,
This bitter cup,
This bitter cup,
Let it pass from me.

Jesus, my sorrowing Jesus,
The sweat like drops of blood upon his brow,
Talking with his Father,
While the three disciples slept,
Saying: Father,
Oh, Father,
Not as I will,
Not as I will,
But let thy will be done.

Oh, look at black-hearted Judas—
Sneaking through the dark of the Garden—
Leading his crucifying mob.
Oh, God!
Strike him down!
Why *don't* you strike him down,

Before he plants his traitor's kiss
Upon my Jesus' cheek?

And they take my blameless Jesus,
And they drag him to the Governor,
To the mighty Roman Governor.
Great Pilate seated in his hall,—
Great Pilate on his judgment seat,
Said: In this man I find no fault.
I find no fault in him.
And Pilate washed his hands.

But they cried out, saying:
Crucify him!—
Crucify him!—
Crucify him!—
His blood be on our heads.
And they beat my loving Jesus,
They spit on my precious Jesus;
They dressed him up in a purple robe,
They put a crown of thorns upon his head,
And they pressed it down—
Oh, they pressed it down—
And they mocked my sweet King Jesus.

Up Golgotha's rugged road
I see my Jesus go.
I see him sink beneath the load,
I see my drooping Jesus sink.
And then they laid hold on Simon,
Black Simon, yes, black Simon;
They put the cross on Simon,
And Simon bore the cross.

On Calvary, on Calvary,
They crucified my Jesus.
They nailed him to the cruel tree,
And the hammer!

The hammer!
The hammer!
Rang through Jerusalem's streets.
The hammer!
The hammer!
The hammer!
Rang through Jerusalem's streets.

Jesus, my lamb-like Jesus,
Shivering as the nails go through his hands;
Jesus, my lamb-like Jesus,
Shivering as the nails go through his feet.
Jesus, my darling Jesus,
Groaning as the Roman spear plunged in his side;
Jesus, my darling Jesus,
Groaning as the blood came spurting from his wound.
Oh, look how they done my Jesus.

Mary,
Weeping Mary,
Sees her poor little Jesus on the cross.
Mary,
Weeping Mary,
Sees her sweet, baby Jesus on the cruel cross,
Hanging between two thieves.

And Jesus, my lonesome Jesus,
Called out once more to his Father,
Saying:
My God,
My God,
Why hast thou forsaken me?
And he drooped his head and died.

And the veil of the temple was split in two,
The midday sun refused to shine,
The thunder rumbled and the lightning wrote
An unknown language in the sky.

What a day! Lord, what a day!
When my blessed Jesus died.

Oh, I tremble, yes, I tremble,
It causes me to tremble, tremble,
When I think how Jesus died;
Died on the steeps of Calvary,
How Jesus died for sinners,
Sinners like you and me.

Let My People Go

And God called Moses from the burning bush,
He called in a still, small voice,
And he said: Moses—Moses—
And Moses listened,
And he answered and said:
Lord, here am I.

And the voice in the bush said: Moses,
Draw not nigh, take off your shoes,
For you're standing on holy ground.
And Moses stopped where he stood,
And Moses took off his shoes,
And Moses looked at the burning bush,
And he heard the voice,
But he saw no man.

Then God again spoke to Moses,
And he spoke in a voice of thunder:
I am the Lord God Almighty,
I am the God of thy fathers,
I am the God of Abraham,
Of Isaac and of Jacob.
And Moses hid his face.

And God said to Moses:
I've seen the awful suffering
Of my people down in Egypt.
I've watched their hard oppressors,
Their overseers and drivers;
The groans of my people have filled my ears
And I can't stand it no longer;
So I'm come down to deliver them
Out of the land of Egypt,
And I will bring them out of that land
Into the land of Canaan;

Therefore, Moses, go down,
Go down into Egypt,
And tell Old Pharaoh
To let my people go.

And Moses said: Lord, who am I
To make a speech before Pharaoh?
For, Lord, you know I'm slow of tongue.
But God said: I will be thy mouth and I will be thy tongue;
Therefore, Moses, go down,
Go down yonder into Egypt land,
And tell Old Pharaoh
To let my people go.

And Moses with his rod in hand
Went down and said to Pharaoh:
Thus saith the Lord God of Israel,
Let my people go.

And Pharaoh looked at Moses,
He stopped still and looked at Moses;
And he said to Moses: Who is this Lord?
I know all the gods of Egypt,
But I know no God of Israel;
So go back, Moses, and tell your God,
I will not let this people go.

Poor Old Pharaoh,
He knows all the knowledge of Egypt,
Yet never knew—
He never knew
The one and the living God.
Poor Old Pharaoh,
He's got all the power of Egypt,
And he's going to try
To test his strength
With the might of the great Jehovah,

With the might of the Lord God of Hosts,
The Lord mighty in battle.
And God, sitting high up in his heaven,
Laughed at poor Old Pharaoh.

And Pharaoh called the overseers,
And Pharaoh called the drivers,
And he said: Put heavier burdens still
On the backs of the Hebrew Children.
Then the people chode with Moses,
And they cried out: Look here, Moses,
You've been to Pharaoh, but look and see
What Pharaoh's done to us now.
And Moses was troubled in mind.

But God said: Go again, Moses,
You and your brother, Aaron,
And say once more to Pharaoh,
Thus saith the Lord God of the Hebrews,
Let my people go.
And Moses and Aaron with their rods in hand
Worked many signs and wonders.
But Pharaoh called for his magic men,
And they worked wonders, too.
So Pharaoh's heart was hardened,
And he would not,
No, he would not
Let God's people go.

And God rained down plagues on Egypt,
Plagues of frogs and lice and locusts,
Plagues of blood and boils and darkness,
And other plagues besides.
But ev'ry time God moved the plague
Old Pharaoh's heart was hardened,
And he would not,
No, he would not

Let God's people go.
And Moses was troubled in mind.

Then the Lord said: Listen, Moses,
The God of Israel will not be mocked,
Just one more witness of my power
I'll give hard-hearted Pharaoh.
This very night about midnight,
I'll pass over Egypt land,
In my righteous wrath will I pass over,
And smite their first-born dead.

And God that night passed over.
And a cry went up out of Egypt.
And Pharaoh rose in the middle of the night
And he sent in a hurry for Moses;
And he said: Go forth from among my people,
You and all the Hebrew Children;
Take your goods and take your flocks,
And get away from the land of Egypt.

And, right then, Moses led them out,
With all their goods and all their flocks;
And God went on before,
A guiding pillar of cloud by day,
And a pillar of fire by night.
And they journeyed on in the wilderness,
And came down to the Red Sea.

In the morning,
Oh, in the morning,
They missed the Hebrew Children.
Four hundred years,
Four hundred years
They'd held them down in Egypt land.
Held them under the driver's lash,
Working without money and without price.

And it might have been Pharaoh's wife that said:
Pharaoh—look what you've done.
You let those Hebrew Children go,
And who's going to serve us now?
Who's going to make our bricks and mortar?
Who's going to plant and plow our corn?
Who's going to get up in the chill of the morning?
And who's going to work in the blazing sun?
Pharaoh, tell me that!

And Pharaoh called his generals,
And the generals called the captains,
And the captains called the soldiers.
And they hitched up all the chariots,
Six hundred chosen chariots of war,
And twenty-four hundred horses.
And the chariots all were full of men,
With swords and shields
And shiny spears
And battle bows and arrows.
And Pharaoh and his army
Pursued the Hebrew Children
To the edge of the Red Sea.

Now, the Children of Israel, looking back,
Saw Pharaoh's army coming.
And the rumble of the chariots was like a thunder storm,
And the whirring of the wheels was like a rushing wind,
And the dust from the horses made a cloud that darked the day,
And the glittering of the spears was like lightnings in the night.

And the Children of Israel all lost faith,
The children of Israel all lost hope;
Deep Red Sea in front of them
And Pharaoh's host behind.
And they mumbled and grumbled among themselves:
Were there no graves in Egypt?

And they wailed aloud to Moses and said:
Slavery in Egypt was better than to come
To die here in this wilderness.

But Moses said:
Stand still! Stand still!
And see the Lord's salvation.
For the Lord God of Israel
Will not forsake his people.
The Lord will break the chariots,
The Lord will break the horsemen,
He'll break great Egypt's sword and shield,
The battle bows and arrows;
This day he'll make proud Pharaoh know
Who is the God of Israel.

And Moses lifted up his rod
Over the Red Sea;
And God with a blast of his nostrils
Blew the waters apart,
And the waves rolled back and stood up in a pile,
And left a path through the middle of the sea
Dry as the sands of the desert.
And the Children of Israel all crossed over
On to the other side.

When Pharaoh saw them crossing dry,
He dashed on in behind them—
Old Pharaoh got about half way cross,
And God unlashed the waters,
And the waves rushed back together,
And Pharaoh and all his army got lost,
And all his host got drownded.
And Moses sang and Miriam danced,
And the people shouted for joy,
And God led the Hebrew Children on
Till they reached the promised land.

Listen!—Listen!
All you sons of Pharaoh.
Who do you think can hold God's people
When the Lord God himself has said,
Let my people go?

The Judgment Day

In that great day,
People, in that great day,
God's a-going to rain down fire.
God's a-going to sit in the middle of the air
To judge the quick and the dead.

Early one of these mornings,
God's a-going to call for Gabriel,
That tall, bright angel, Gabriel;
And God's a-going to say to him: Gabriel,
Blow your silver trumpet,
And wake the living nations.

And Gabriel's going to ask him: Lord,
How loud must I blow it?
And God's a-going to tell him: Gabriel,
Blow it calm and easy.
Then putting one foot on the mountain top,
And the other in the middle of the sea,
Gabriel's going to stand and blow his horn,
To wake the living nations.

Then God's a-going to say to him: Gabriel,
Once more blow your silver trumpet,
And wake the nations underground.

And Gabriel's going to ask him: Lord
How loud must I blow it?
And God's a-going to tell him: Gabriel,
Like seven peals of thunder.
Then the tall, bright angel, Gabriel,
Will put one foot on the battlements of heaven
And the other on the steps of hell,
And blow that silver trumpet
Till he shakes old hell's foundations.

And I feel Old Earth a-shuddering—
And I see the graves a-bursting—
And I hear a sound,
A blood-chilling sound.
What sound is that I hear?
It's the clicking together of the dry bones,
Bone to bone—the dry bones.
And I see coming out of the bursting graves,
And marching up from the valley of death,
The army of the dead.

And the living and the dead in the twinkling of an eye
Are caught up in the middle of the air,
Before God's judgment bar.

Oh-o-oh, sinner,
Where will you stand,
In that great day when God's a-going to rain down fire?
Oh, you gambling man—where will you stand?
You whore-mongering man—where will you stand?
Liars and backsliders—where will you stand,
In that great day when God's a-going to rain down fire?

And God will divide the sheep from the goats,
The one on the right, the other on the left.
And to them on the right God's a-going to say:
Enter into my kingdom.
And those who've come through great tribulations,
And washed their robes in the blood of the Lamb,
They will enter in—
Clothed in spotless white,
With starry crowns upon their heads,
And silver slippers on their feet,
And harps within their hands;—

And two by two they'll walk
Up and down the golden street,
Feasting on the milk and honey

Singing new songs of Zion,
Chattering with the angels
All around the Great White Throne.

And to them on the left God's a-going to say:
Depart from me into everlasting darkness,
Down into the bottomless pit.
And the wicked like lumps of lead will start to fall,
Headlong for seven days and nights they'll fall,
Plumb into the big, black, red-hot mouth of hell,
Belching out fire and brimstone.
And their cries like howling, yelping dogs,
Will go up with the fire and smoke from hell,
But God will stop his ears.

Too late, sinner! Too late!
Good-bye, sinner! Good-bye!
In hell, sinner! In hell!
Beyond the reach of the love of God.

And I hear a voice, crying, crying:
Time shall be no more!
Time shall be no more!
Time shall be no more!
And the sun will go out like a candle in the wind,
The moon will turn to dripping blood,
The stars will fall like cinders,
And the sea will burn like tar;
And the earth shall melt away and be dissolved,
And the sky will roll up like a scroll.
With a wave of his hand God will blot out time,
And start the wheel of eternity.

Sinner, oh, sinner,
Where will you stand
In that great day when God's a-going to rain down fire?

PART II

Saint Peter Relates an Incident
and
Fifty Years and Other Poems

JAMES WELDON JOHNSON *published* Saint Peter Relates an Incident *in 1935. In this volume he integrates the feelings and forces of black life with general themes.*

We can identify two types of poetry here: The poetry of the first type manifests protest, challenge, and hope. The poems of the second type, including "Mother, Farewell!," "My City," and "Girl of Fifteen," are not imbued with the polemical aspects of the race problem. The sentiments expressed in these poems are common to all humankind.

Johnson's protest poems represent the union of his political experience and his creative talent. As an anti-lynching crusader in the early civil rights movement, Johnson wrote the poem "Brothers" in 1916. Deft in feeling, this poem expresses a dialogue, between the mob and the black victim, that has been going on for three centuries in America. The theme in Johnson's protest poems is his challenge to black America to make this country as much their land as it is the land of white citizens. As he writes in "Fifty Years," "This land is ours by right of birth, / This land is ours by right of toil."

He began writing dialect poems a few years before the onset of the twentieth century but discarded the form about 1910. (He had also experimented with dialect during his college years, 1890–94.) Initially reluctant to publish his dialect poems, he quickly realized that the attempt to exclude them from American literature would be both a racial and a national loss.

Johnson's most famous poem, "Lift Every Voice and Sing," is included in this section. Written in 1900 and set to music by his brother J. Rosamond Johnson, the song was originally called the "Negro National Hymn." By the 1920s

African Americans had made the song their national anthem. "Lift Every Voice and Sing" embodies the history, hopes, and aspirations of African Americans in this nation. "Nothing that I have done has paid me back so fully in satisfaction as being part creator of this song," he wrote.

Saint Peter Relates an Incident
of the Resurrection Day

Eternities—now numbering six or seven—
Hung heavy on the hands of all in heaven.
Archangels tall and fair had reached the stage
Where they began to show some signs of age.

The faces of the flaming seraphim
Were slightly drawn, their eyes were slightly dim.
The cherubs, too, for now—oh, an infinite while
Had worn but a wistful shade of their dimpling smile.

The serried singers of the celestial choir
Disclosed a woeful want of pristine fire;
When they essayed to strike the glad refrain,
Their attack was weak, their tone revealed voice strain.

Their expression seemed to say, "We must! We must!" though
'Twas more than evident they lacked the gusto;
It could not be elsewise—that fact all can agree on—
Chanting the selfsame choral æon after æon.

Thus was it that Saint Peter at the gate
Began a brand new thing in heaven: to relate
Some reminiscences from heavenly history,
Which had till then been more or less a mystery.

So now and then, by turning back the pages,
Were whiled away some moments from the ages,
Was gained a respite from the monotony
That can't help settling on eternity.

II

Now, there had been a lapse of ages hoary,
And the angels clamored for another story.

"Tell us a tale, Saint Peter," they entreated;
And gathered close around where he was seated.

Saint Peter stroked his beard,
And "Yes," he said
By the twinkle in his eye
And the nodding of his head.

A moment brief he fumbled with his keys—
It seemed to help him call up memories—
Straightway there flashed across his mind the one
About the unknown soldier
Who came from Washington.

The hosts stood listening,
Breathlessly awake;
And thus Saint Peter spake:

III

'Twas Resurrection morn,
And Gabriel blew a blast upon his horn
That echoed through the arches high and vast
Of Time and Space—a long resounding blast

To wake the dead, dead for a million years;
A blast to reach and pierce their dust-stopped ears;
To quicken them, wherever they might be,
Deep in the earth or deeper in the sea.

A shudder shook the world, and gaping graves
Gave up their dead. Out from the parted waves
Came the prisoners of old ocean. The dead belonging
To every land and clime came thronging.

From the four corners of all the earth they drew,
Their faces radiant and their bodies new.

Creation pulsed and swayed beneath the tread
Of all the living, and all the risen dead.

Swift-winged heralds of heaven flew back and forth,
Out of the east, to the south, the west, the north,
Giving out quick commands, and yet benign,
Marshaling the swarming milliards into line.

The recording angel in words of thundering might,
At which the timid, doubting souls took fright,
Bade all to await the grand roll-call; to wit,
To see if in the Book their names were writ.

The multitudinous business of the day
Progressed, but naturally, not without delay.
Meanwhile, within the great American border
There was the issuance of a special order.

IV

The word went forth, spoke by some grand panjandrum,
Perhaps, by some high potentate of Klandom,
That all the trusty patriotic mentors,
And duly qualified Hundred-Percenters

Should forthwith gather together upon the banks
Of the Potomac, there to form their ranks,
March to the tomb, by orders to be given,
And escort the unknown soldier up to heaven.

Compliantly they gathered from each region,
The G.A.R., the D.A.R., the Legion,
Veterans of wars—Mexican, Spanish, Haitian—
Trustees of the patriotism of the nation;

Key Men, Watchmen, shunning circumlocution,
The Sons of the This and That and of the Revolution;

Not to forget, there gathered every man
Of the Confederate Veterans and the Ku-Klux Klan.

The Grand Imperial Marshal gave the sign;
Column on column, the marchers fell in line;
Majestic as an army in review,
They swept up Washington's wide avenue.

Then, through the long line ran a sudden flurry,
The marchers in the rear began to hurry;
They feared unless the procession hastened on,
The unknown soldier might be risen and gone.

The fear was groundless; when they arrived, in fact,
They found the grave entirely intact.
(Resurrection plans were long, long past completing
Ere there was thought of re-enforced concreting.)

They heard a faint commotion in the tomb,
Like the stirring of a child within the womb;
At once they saw the plight, and set about
The job to dig the unknown soldier out.

They worked away, they labored with a will,
They toiled with pick, with crowbar, and with drill
To cleave a breach; nor did the soldier shirk;
Within his limits, he helped to push the work.

He, underneath the débris, heaved and hove
Up toward the opening which they cleaved and clove;
Through it, at last, his towering form loomed big and bigger—
"Great God Almighty! Look!" they cried, "he is a nigger!"

Surprise and consternation and dismay
Swept over the crowd; none knew just what to say
Or what to do. And all fell back aghast.
Silence—but only an instant did it last.

Bedlam: They clamored, they railed, some roared, some bleated;
All of them felt that somehow they'd been cheated.
The question rose: What to do with him, then?
The Klan was all for burying him again.

The scheme involved within the Klan's suggestion
Gave rise to a rather nice metaphysical question:
Could he be forced again through death's dark portal,
Since now his body and soul were both immortal?

Would he, forsooth, the curious-minded queried,
Even in concrete, re-entombed, stay buried?
In a moment more, midst the pile of broken stone,
The unknown soldier stood, and stood alone.

V

The day came to a close.
And heaven—hell too—was filled with them that rose.
I shut the pearly gate and turned the key;
For Time was now merged into Eternity.

I gave one last look over the jasper wall,
And afar descried a figure dark and tall:
The unknown soldier, dust-stained and begrimed,
Climbing his way to heaven, and singing as he climbed:
  Deep river, my home is over Jordan,
  Deep river, I want to cross over into camp-ground.

Climbing and singing—
  Deep river, my home is over Jordan,
  Deep river, I want to cross over into camp-ground.

Nearer and louder—
  Deep river, my home is over Jordan,
  Deep river, I want to cross over into camp-ground.

At the jasper wall—
   Deep river, my home is over Jordan,
   Deep river,
   Lord,
   I want to cross over into camp-ground.

I rushed to the gate and flung it wide,
Singing, he entered with a loose, long stride;
Singing and swinging up the golden street,
The music married to the tramping of his feet.
Tall, black soldier-angel marching alone,
Swinging up the golden street, saluting at the great white throne.
Singing, singing, singing, singing clear and strong.
Singing, singing, singing, till heaven took up the song:
   Deep river, my home is over Jordan,
   Deep river, I want to cross over into camp-ground.

   VI

The tale was done,
The angelic hosts dispersed,
   but not till after
There ran through heaven
Something that quivered
   'twixt tears and laughter.

O Black and Unknown Bards

O black and unknown bards of long ago,
How came your lips to touch the sacred fire?
How, in your darkness, did you come to know
The power and beauty of the minstrel's lyre?
Who first from midst his bonds lifted his eyes?
Who first from out the still watch, lone and long,
Feeling the ancient faith of prophets rise
Within his dark-kept soul, burst into song?

Heart of what slave poured out such melody
As "Steal Away to Jesus"? On its strains
His spirit must have nightly floated free,
Though still about his hands he felt his chains.
Who heard great "Jordan roll"? Whose starward eye
Saw chariot "swing low"? And who was he
That breathed that comforting, melodic sigh,
"Nobody Knows de Trouble I See"?

What merely living clod, what captive thing,
Could up toward God through all its darkness grope,
And find within its deadened heart to sing
These songs of sorrow, love, and faith, and hope?
How did it catch that subtle undertone,
That note in music heard not with the ears?
How sound the elusive reed so seldom blown,
Which stirs the soul or melts the heart to tears?

Not that great German master in his dream
Of harmonies that thundered amongst the stars
At the creation, ever heard a theme
Nobler than "Go Down, Moses." Mark its bars,
How like a mighty trumpet-call they stir
The blood. Such are the notes that men have sung
Going to valorous deeds; such tones there were
That helped make history when Time was young.

There is a wide, wide wonder in it all,
That from degraded rest and servile toil
The fiery spirit of the seer should call
These simple children of the sun and soil.
O black slave singers, gone, forgot, unfamed,
You—you alone, of all the long, long line
Of those who've sung untaught, unknown, unnamed,
Have stretched out upward, seeking the divine.

You sang not deeds of heroes or of kings;
No chant of bloody war, no exulting pæan
Of arms-won triumphs; but your humble strings
You touched in chord with music empyrean.
You sang far better than you knew; the songs
That for your listeners' hungry hearts sufficed
Still live—but more than this to you belongs:
You sang a race from wood and stone to Christ.

Brothers—American Drama

(THE MOB SPEAKS:)
 See! There he stands; not brave, but with an air
 Of sullen stupor. Mark him well! Is he
 Not more like brute than man? Look in his eye!
 No light is there; none, save the glint that shines
 In the now glaring, and now shifting orbs
 Of some wild animal caught in the hunter's trap.

 How came this beast in human shape and form?
 Speak man!—We call you man because you wear
 His shape—How are you thus? Are you not from
 That docile, child-like, tender-hearted race
 Which we have known three centuries? Not from
 That more than faithful race which through three wars
 Fed our dear wives and nursed our helpless babes
 Without a single breach of trust? Speak out!

(THE VICTIM SPEAKS:)
 I am, and am not.

(THE MOB SPEAKS AGAIN:)
       Then who, why are you?

(THE VICTIM SPEAKS AGAIN:)
 I am a thing not new, I am as old
 As human nature. I am that which lurks,
 Ready to spring whenever a bar is loosed;
 The ancient trait which fights incessantly
 Against restraint, balks at the upward climb;
 The weight forever seeking to obey
 The law of downward pull—and I am more:
 The bitter fruit am I of planted seed;
 The resultant, the inevitable end
 Of evil forces and the powers of wrong.

Lessons in degradation, taught and learned,
The memories of cruel sights and deeds,
The pent-up bitterness, the unspent hate
Filtered through fifteen generations have
Sprung up and found in me sporadic life.
In me the muttered curse of dying men,
On me the stain of conquered women, and
Consuming me the fearful fires of lust,
Lit long ago, by other hands than mine.
In me the down-crushed spirit, the hurled-back prayers
Of wretches now long dead—their dire bequests.
In me the echo of the stifled cry
Of children for their battered mothers' breasts.

I claim no race, no race claims me; I am
No more than human dregs; degenerate;
The monstrous offspring of the monster, Sin;
I am—just what I am. . . . The race that fed
Your wives and nursed your babes would do the same
Today. But I—

(THE MOB CONCLUDES:)
                    Enough, the brute must die!
Quick! Chain him to that oak! It will resist
The fire much longer than this slender pine.
Now bring the fuel! Pile it round him! Wait!
Pile not so fast or high! or we shall lose
The agony and terror in his face.
And now the torch! Good fuel that! the flames
Already leap head-high. Ha! hear that shriek!
And there's another! wilder than the first.
Fetch water! Water! Pour a little on
The fire, lest it should burn too fast. Hold so!
Now let it slowly blaze again. See there!
He squirms! He groans! His eyes bulge wildly out,
Searching around in vain appeal for help!
Another shriek, the last! Watch how the flesh
Grows crisp and hangs till, turned to ash, it sifts

Down through the coils of chain that hold erect
The ghastly frame against the bark-scorched tree.

Stop! to each man no more than one man's share.
You take that bone, and you this tooth; the chain,
Let us divide its links; this skull, of course,
In fair division, to the leader comes.

And now his fiendish crime has been avenged;
Let us back to our wives and children—say,
What did he mean by those last muttered words,
"Brothers in spirit, brothers in deed are we"?

O Southland!

O Southland! O Southland!
  Have you not heard the call,
The trumpet blown, the word made known
  To the nations, one and all?
The watchword, the hope-word,
  Salvation's present plan?
A gospel new, for all—for you:
  Man shall be saved by man.

O Southland! O Southland!
  Do you not hear today
The mighty beat of onward feet,
  And know you not their way?
'Tis forward, 'tis upward,
  On to the fair white arch
Of Freedom's dome, and there is room
  For each man who would march.

O Southland, fair Southland!
  Then why do you still cling
To an idle age and a musty page,
  To a dead and useless thing?
'Tis springtime! 'Tis work-time!
  The world is young again!
And God's above, and God is love,
  And men are only men.

We to America

How would you have us, as we are—
Or sinking 'neath the load we bear?
Our eyes fixed forward on a star—
Or gazing empty at despair?

Rising or falling? Men or things?
With dragging pace or footsteps fleet?
Strong, willing sinews in your wings?
Or tightening chains about your feet?

Mother Night

Eternities before the first-born day,
    Or ere the first sun fledged his wings of flame,
    Calm Night, the everlasting and the same,
    A brooding mother over chaos lay.
And whirling suns shall blaze and then decay,
    Shall run their fiery courses and then claim
    The haven of the darkness whence they came;
    Back to Nirvanic peace shall grope their way.

So when my feeble sun of life burns out,
    And sounded is the hour for my long sleep,
    I shall, full weary of the feverish light,
Welcome the darkness without fear or doubt,
    And heavy-lidded, I shall softly creep
    Into the quiet bosom of the Night.

The Young Warrior

Mother, shed no mournful tears,
But gird me on my sword;
And give no utterance to thy fears,
But bless me with thy word.

The lines are drawn! The fight is on!
A cause is to be won!
Mother, look not so paled and wan;
Give Godspeed to thy son.

Now let thine eyes my way pursue
Where'er my footsteps fare;
And when they lead beyond thy view,
Send after me a prayer.

But pray not to defend from harm,
Nor danger to dispel;
Pray, rather, that with steadfast arm
I fight the battle well.

Pray, mother of mine, that I always keep
My heart and purpose strong,
My sword unsullied and ready to leap
Unsheathed against the wrong.

The White Witch

O brothers mine, take care! Take care!
The great white witch rides out tonight,
Trust not your prowess nor your strength;
Your only safety lies in flight;
For in her glance there is a snare,
And in her smile there is a blight.

The great white witch you have not seen?
Then, younger brothers mine, forsooth,
Like nursery children you have looked
For ancient hag and snaggle-tooth;
But no, not so; the witch appears
In all the glowing charms of youth.

Her lips are like carnations red,
Her face like new-born lilies fair,
Her eyes like ocean waters blue,
She moves with subtle grace and air,
And all about her head there floats
The golden glory of her hair.

But though she always thus appears
In form of youth and mood of mirth,
Unnumbered centuries are hers,
The infant planets saw her birth;
The child of throbbing Life is she,
Twin sister to the greedy earth.

And back behind those smiling lips,
And down within those laughing eyes,
And underneath the soft caress
Of hand and voice and purring sighs,
The shadow of the panther lurks,
The spirit of the vampire lies.

For I have seen the great white witch,
And she has led me to her lair,
And I have kissed her red, red lips
And cruel face so white and fair;
Around me she has twined her arms,
And bound me with her yellow hair.

I felt those red lips burn and sear
My body like a living coal;
Obeyed the power of those eyes
As the needle trembles to the pole;
And did not care although I felt
The strength go ebbing from my soul.

Oh! she has seen your strong young limbs,
And heard your laughter loud and gay,
And in your voices she has caught
The echo of a far-off day,
When man was closer to the earth;
And she has marked you for her prey.

She feels the old Antæan strength
In you, the great dynamic beat
Of primal passions, and she sees
In you the last besieged retreat
Of love relentless, lusty, fierce,
Love pain-ecstatic, cruel-sweet.

O, brothers mine, take care! Take care!
The great white witch rides out tonight.
O, younger brothers mine, beware!
Look not upon her beauty bright;
For in her glance there is a snare,
And in her smile there is a blight.

My City

When I come down to sleep death's endless night,
The threshold of the unknown dark to cross,
What to me then will be the keenest loss,
When this bright world blurs on my fading sight?
Will it be that no more I shall see the trees
Or smell the flowers or hear the singing birds
Or watch the flashing streams or patient herds?
No. I am sure it will be none of these.

But, ah! Manhattan's sights and sounds, her smells,
Her crowds, her throbbing force, the thrill that comes
From being of her a part, her subtle spells,
Her shining towers, her avenues, her slums—
O God! the stark, unutterable pity,
To be dead, and never again behold my city.

The Glory of the Day Was in Her Face

The glory of the day was in her face,
The beauty of the night was in her eyes.
And over all her loveliness, the grace
Of morning blushing in the early skies.

And in her voice, the calling of the dove;
Like music of a sweet, melodious part.
And in her smile, the breaking light of love;
And all the gentle virtues in her heart.

And now the glorious day, the beauteous night,
The birds that signal to their mates at dawn,
To my dull ears, to my tear-blinded sight
Are one with all the dead, since she is gone.

Life

Out of the infinite sea of eternity
To climb, and for an instant stand
Upon an island speck of time.

From the impassible peace of the darkness
To wake, and blink at the garish light
Through one short space of fretfulness.

The Black Mammy

O whitened head entwined in turban gay,
O kind black face, O crude, but tender hand,
O foster-mother in whose arms there lay
The race whose sons are masters of the land!
It was thine arms that sheltered in their fold,
It was thine eyes that followed through the length
Of infant days these sons. In times of old
It was thy breast that nourished them to strength.

So often hast thou to thy bosom pressed
The golden head, the face and brow of snow;
So often has it 'gainst thy broad, dark breast
Lain, set off like a quickened cameo.
Thou simple soul, as cuddling down that babe
With thy sweet croon, so plaintive and so wild,
Came ne'er the thought to thee, swift like a stab,
That it some day might crush thy own black child?

Fragment

The hand of Fate cannot be stayed,
The course of Fate cannot be steered,
By all the gods that man has made,
Nor all the devils he has feared,
Not by the prayers that might be prayed
In all the temples he has reared.

See! In your very midst there dwell
Ten thousand thousand blacks, a wedge
Forged in the furnaces of hell,
And sharpened to a cruel edge
By wrong and by injustice fell,
And driven by hatred as a sledge.

A wedge so slender at the start—
Just twenty slaves in shackles bound—
And yet which split the land apart
With shrieks of war and battle sound,
Which pierced the nation's very heart,
And still lies cankering in the wound.

Not all the glory of your pride,
Preserved in story and in song,
Can from the judging future hide,
Through all the coming ages long,
That though you bravely fought and died,
You fought and died for what was wrong.

'Tis fixed—for them that violate
The eternal laws, naught shall avail
Till they their error expiate;
Nor shall their unborn children fail
To pay the full required weight
Into God's great, unerring scale.

Think not repentance can redeem,
That sin his wages can withdraw;
No, think as well to change the scheme
Of worlds that move in reverent awe;
Forgiveness is an idle dream,
God is not love, no, God is law.

Mother, Farewell!

(From the Spanish of Plácido. Written in the chapel of
the Hospital de Santa Cristina on the night before his
execution.)

If the unfortunate fate engulfing me,
The ending of my history of grief,
The closing of my span of years so brief,
Mother, should wake a single pang in thee,
Weep not. No saddening thought to me devote;
I calmly go to a death that is glory-filled;
My lyre before it is forever stilled
Breathes out to thee its last and dying note.

A note scarce more than a burden-easing sigh,
Tender and sacred, innocent, sincere,
Spontaneous and instinctive as the cry
I gave at birth. And now the hour is here—
O God, thy mantle of mercy over my sins!
Mother, farewell! The pilgrimage begins.

Girl of Fifteen

Girl of fifteen,
I see you each morning from my window
As you pass on your way to school.
I do more than see, I watch you.
I furtively draw the curtain aside.
And my heart leaps through my eyes
And follows you down the street;
Leaving me behind, half-hid
And wholly ashamed.

What holds me back,
Half-hid behind the curtains and wholly ashamed,
But my forty years beyond your fifteen?

Girl of fifteen, as you pass
There passes, too, a lightning flash of time
In which you lift those forty summers off my head,
And take those forty winters out of my heart.

The Suicide

For fifty years,
Cruel, insatiable old World,
You have punched me over the heart
Till you made me cough blood.
The few paltry things I gathered
You snatched out of my hands.
You have knocked the cup from my thirsty lips.
You have laughed at my hunger of body and soul.

You look at me now and think,
"He is still strong,
There ought to be twenty more years of good punching there.
At the end of that time he will be old and broken,
Not able to strike back,
But cringing and crying for leave
To live a little longer."

Those twenty, pitiful, extra years
Would please you more than the fifty past,
Would they not, old World?
Well, I hold them up before your greedy eyes,
And snatch them away as I laugh in your face.
Ha—

Down by the Carib Sea

I

Sunrise in the Tropics

Sol, Sol, mighty lord of the tropic zone,
Here I wait with the trembling stars
To see thee once more take thy throne.

There the patient palm tree watching
Waits to say "Good morn" to thee,
And a throb of expectation
Pulses through the earth and me.

Now over nature falls a hush,
Look! the east is all a-blush;
And a growing crimson crest
Dims the late stars in the west;
Now, a wave of vivid light
Sweeps away the shimmering night.
See! the miracle is done!
Once more behold, the Sun!

II

Los Cigarrillos

This is the land of the dark-eyed *gente*,
Of the *dolce far niente*,
Where we dream away
Both the night and day.
At night-time in sleep our dreams we invoke,
Our dreams come by day through the redolent smoke,
As it lazily curls,
And slowly unfurls
From our lips,
And the tips

Of our fragrant *cigarillos.*
For life in the tropics is only a joke,
So we pass it in dreams, and we pass it in smoke,
Smoke—smoke—smoke.

Tropical constitutions
Call for occasional revolutions,
But after that's through,
Why there's nothing to do
But smoke—smoke;

For life in the tropics is only a joke,
So we pass it in dreams, and we pass it in smoke,
Smoke—smoke—smoke.

III

*Teestay**

Of tropic sensations, the worst
Is, *sin duda,* the tropical thirst.
When it starts in your throat and constantly grows,
Till you feel that it reaches down to your toes,
When your mouth tastes like fur
And your tongue turns to dust,
There's but one thing to do,
And do it you must,
Drink *teestay.*

Teestay, a drink with a history,
A delicious, delectable mystery,
"*Cinco centavos el vaso, señor,*
If you take one, you will surely want more."

Teestay, teestay,
The national drink on a feast day;

Tiste is a popular drink in Nicaragua.

How it coolingly tickles,
As downward it trickles,
Teestay, teestay.

And you wish, as you take it down at a quaff,
That your neck was constructed à la giraffe.
Teestay, teestay.

IV

The Lottery Girl

"Lottery, lottery,
Take a chance at the lottery?
Take a ticket,
Or, better, take two;
Who knows what the future
May hold for you?
Lottery, lottery,
Take a chance at the lottery?"

Oh, limpid-eyed girl,
I would take every chance,
If only the prize
Were a love-flashing glance
From your fathomless eyes.

"Lottery, lottery,
Try your luck at the lottery?
Consider the size
Of the capital prize,
And take tickets
For the lottery.
Tickets, *señor?* Tickets, *señor?*
Take a chance at the lottery?"

Oh, crimson-lipped girl,
With the magical smile,

I would count that the gamble
Were well worth the while,
Not a chance would I miss,
If only the prize
Were a honey-bee kiss
Gathered in sips
From those full-ripened lips,
And a love-flashing glance
From your eyes.

V

The Dancing Girl

Do you know what it is to dance?
Perhaps, you do know, in a fashion;
But by dancing I mean,
Not what's generally seen,
But dancing of fire and passion,
Of fire and delirious passion.

With a dusky-haired *señorita*,
Her dark, misty eyes near your own,
And her scarlet-red mouth,
Like a rose of the south,
The reddest that ever was grown,
So close that you catch
Her quick-panting breath
As across your own face it is blown,
With a sigh, and a moan.

Ah! that is dancing,
As here by the Carib it's known.

Now, whirling and twirling
Like furies we go;
Now, soft and caressing
And sinuously slow;

With an undulating motion,
Like waves on a breeze-kissed ocean—
And the scarlet-red mouth
Is nearer your own,
And the dark, misty eyes
Still softer have grown.

Ah! that is dancing, that is dancing,
As here by the Carib it's known.

VI

Sunset in the Tropics

A silver flash from the sinking sun,
Then a shot of crimson across the sky
That, bursting, lets a thousand colors fly
And riot among the clouds; they run,
Deepening in purple, flaming in gold,
Changing, and opening fold after fold,
Then fading through all of the tints of the rose into gray,
Till, taking quick fright at the coming night,
They rush out down the west,
In hurried quest
Of the fleeing day.

Now above, where the tardiest color flares a moment yet,
One point of light, now two, now three are set
To form the starry stairs—
And, in her firefly crown,
Queen Night, on velvet slippered feet, comes softly down.

Deep in the Quiet Wood

Are you bowed down in heart?
Do you but hear the clashing discords and the din of life?
Then come away, come to the peaceful wood.
Here bathe your soul in silence. Listen! Now,
From out the palpitating solitude
Do you not catch, yet faint, elusive strains?
They are above, around, within you, everywhere.
Silently listen! Clear, and still more clear, they come.
They bubble up in rippling notes, and swell in singing tones.
Now let your soul run the whole gamut of the wondrous scale
Until, responsive to the tonic chord,
It touches the diapason of God's grand cathedral organ,
Filling earth for you with heavenly peace
And holy harmonies.

Prayer at Sunrise

O mighty, powerful, dark-dispelling sun,
Now thou art risen, and thy day begun.
How shrink the shrouding mists before thy face,
As up thou spring'st to thy diurnal race!
How darkness chases darkness to the west,
As shades of light on light rise radiant from thy crest!
For thee, great source of strength, emblem of might,
In hours of darkest gloom there is no night.
Thou shinest on though clouds hide thee from sight,
And through each break thou sendest down thy light.

O greater Maker of this Thy great sun,
Give me the strength this one day's race to run;
Fill me with light, fill me with sun-like strength;
Fill me with joy to rob the day its length.
Light from within, light that will outward shine,
Strength to make strong some weaker heart than mine,
Joy to make glad each soul that feels its touch;
Great Father of the sun, I ask this much.

Her Eyes Twin Pools

Her eyes, twin pools of mystic light,
The blend of star-sheen and black night;
O'er which, to sound their glamouring haze,
A man might bend, and vainly gaze.

Her eyes, twin pools so dark and deep,
In which life's ancient mysteries sleep;
Wherein, to seek the quested goal,
A man might plunge, and lose his soul.

Vashti

I sometimes take you in my dreams to a far-off land I used to
    know,
Back in the ages long ago; a land of palms and languid streams.

A land, by night, of jeweled skies, by day, of shores that
    glistened bright,
Within whose arms, outstretched and white, a sapphire sea lay
    crescent-wise.

Where twilight fell like silver floss, where rose the golden moon
    half-hid
Behind a shadowy pyramid; a land beneath the Southern Cross.

And there the days dreamed in their flight, each one a poem
    chanted through,
Which at its close was merged into the muted music of the night.

And you were a princess in those days. And I—I was your
    serving lad.
But who ever served with heart so glad, or lived so for a word of
    praise?

And if that word you chanced to speak, how all my senses
    swayed and reeled,
Till low beside your feet I kneeled, with happiness o'erwrought
    and weak.

If, when your golden cup I bore, you deigned to lower your eyes
    to mine,
Eyes cold, yet fervid, like the wine, I knew not how to wish for
    more.

I trembled at the thought to dare to gaze upon, to scrutinize
The deep-sea mystery of your eyes, the sun-lit splendor of your
    hair.

To let my timid glances rest upon you long enough to note
How fair and slender was your throat, how white the promise of
    your breast.

But though I did not dare to chance a lingering look, an open
    gaze
Upon your beauty's blinding rays, I ventured many a stolen
    glance.

I fancy, too (but could not state what trick of mind the fancy
    caused),
At times your eyes upon me paused, and marked my figure lithe
    and straight.

Once when my eyes met yours it seemed that in your cheek,
    despite your pride,
A flush arose and swiftly died; or was it something that I
    dreamed?

Within your radiance like the star of morning, there I stood and
    served,
Close by, unheeded, unobserved. You were so near, and, yet,
    so far.

Ah! just to stretch my hand and touch the musky sandals on
    your feet!—
My breaking heart! of rapture sweet it never could have held so
    much.

Oh, beauty-haunted memory! Your face so proud, your eyes so
    calm,
Your body like a slim young palm, and sinuous as a willow tree.

Caught up beneath your slender arms, and girdled round your
    supple waist,
A robe of curious silk that graced, but only scarce concealed
    your charms.

A golden band about your head, a crimson jewel at your throat
Which, when the sunlight on it smote, turned to a living heart
and bled.

But oh, that mystic bleeding stone, that work of nature's magic
art,
Which mimicked so a wounded heart, could never bleed as did
my own!
. . . .

Now after ages long and sad, in this stern land we meet anew;
No more a princess proud are you, and I—I am no serving lad.

And, yet, dividing us, I meet a wider gulf than that which stood
Between a princess of the blood and him who served low at her
feet.

If I Were Paris

Not for me the budding girl
Or the maiden in full bloom,
Sure of beauty and of charm,
Careless of the distant doom,
Laughing in the face of years
That stretch out so long and far,
Mindful of the things to be,
Heedless of the things that are;

But the woman sweetly ripe,
Under the autumn of her skies;
Thin lines of care about her mouth,
And utterless longings in her eyes.

Ghosts of the Old Year

The snow has ceased its fluttering flight,
The wind sunk to a whisper light,
An ominous stillness fills the night,
    A pause—a hush.
At last, a sound that breaks the spell,
Loud, clanging mouthings of a bell,
That through the silence peal and swell,
    And roll, and rush.

What does this brazen tongue declare,
That falling on the midnight air
Brings to my heart a sense of care
    Akin to fright?
'Tis telling that the year is dead,
The New Year come, the Old-Year fled,
Another leaf before me spread
    On which to write.

It tells of deeds that were not done,
It tells of races never run,
Of victories that were not won,
    Barriers unleaped.
It tells of many a squandered day,
Of slighted gems and treasured clay,
Of precious stores not laid away,
    Of fields unreaped.

And so the years go swiftly by,
Each, coming, brings ambitions high,
And each, departing, leaves a sigh
    Linked to the past.
Large resolutions, little deeds;
Thus, filled with aims unreached, life speeds,
Until the blotted record reads,
    "Failure!" at last.

Beauty Never Old

When buffeted and beaten by life's storms,
When by the bitterness of life oppressed,
I need no surer haven than your arms,
I want no happier shelter than your breast.

When over my way there falls the sudden blight
Of sunless days and nights of starless skies,
Enough for me the ever-steadfast light
I know is always shining in your eyes.

The world, for me,
And all the world can hold
Is circled by your arms;
For me there lies
Within the lighted shadows of your eyes
The only beauty that is never old.

Blessed Sleep

Blessed sleep, kindest minister to man,
Sure and silent distiller of the balm of rest,
Having alone the power, when naught else can,
To soothe the torn and sorrow-ridden breast.
When bleeding hearts no comforter can find,
When burdened souls droop under weight of woe,
When thought is torture to the troubled mind,
When grief-relieving tears refuse to flow,
Respite but comes on sleep's faint-beating wings;
From them oblivion's sweet peace is shed—
But ah, the old pain that the waking brings,
That lives again so soon as sleep is fled.
  Man, why should thought of death cause you to weep,
   Since death is but an endless, dreamless sleep.

The Greatest of These Is War

Around the council-board of hell, with Satan at their head,
The three great scourges of humanity sat.
Gaunt Famine, with hollow cheek and voice, arose and spoke:
"O Prince, I have stalked the earth,
And my victims by ten thousands I have slain.
I have smitten old and young.
Mouths of the helpless old moaning for bread, I have filled with
        dust;
And I have laughed to see a crying babe tug at the shriveling
        breast
Of its mother, dead and cold.
I have heard the cries and prayers of men go up to a tearless sky,
And fall back upon an earth of ashes;
But, heedless, I have gone on with my work.
'Tis thus, O Prince, that I have scourged mankind."

And Satan nodded his head.

Pale Pestilence, with stenchful breath, then spoke and said:
"Great Prince, my brother, Famine, attacks the poor.
He is most terrible against the helpless and the old.
But I have made a charnel-house of the mightiest cities of men.
When I strike, neither their stores of gold or of grain avail.
With a breath I lay low their strongest, and wither up their
        fairest.
I come upon them without warning, lancing invisible death.
From me they flee with eyes and mouths distended;
I poison the air for which they gasp, and I strike them down
        fleeing.
'Tis thus, great Prince, that I have scourged mankind."

And Satan nodded his head.

Then the red monster, War, rose up and spoke;
His blood-shot eyes glared round him, and his thundering voice

Echoed through the murky vaults of hell:
"O, mighty Prince, my brothers, Famine and Pestilence,
Have slain their thousands and ten thousands—true;
But the greater their victories have been,
The more have they wakened in Man's breast
The God-like attributes of sympathy, of brotherhood and love
And made of him a searcher after wisdom.
But I arouse in Man the demon and the brute,
I plant black hatred in his heart and red revenge.
From the summit of fifty thousand years of upward climb
I haul him down to the level of the start, back to the wolf.
I give him claws.
I set his teeth into his brother's throat.
I make him drunk with his brother's blood.
And I laugh ho! ho! while he destroys himself.
O mighty Prince, not only do I slay,
I draw Man hellward."

And Satan smiled, stretched out his hand, and said:
"O War, of all the scourges of humanity, I crown you chief."

And hell rang with the acclamation of the Fiends.

A Poet to His Baby Son

Tiny bit of humanity,
Blessed with your mother's face,
And cursed with your father's mind.

I say cursed with your father's mind,
Because you can lie so long and so quietly on your back,
Playing with the dimpled big toe of your left foot,
And looking away,
Through the ceiling of the room, and beyond.
Can it be that already you are thinking of being a poet?

Why don't you kick and howl,
And make the neighbors talk about
"That damned baby next door,"
And make up your mind forthwith
To grow up and be a banker
Or a politician or some other sort of go-getter
Or—?—whatever you decide upon,
Rid yourself of these incipient thoughts
About being a poet.

For poets no longer are makers of songs,
Chanters of the gold and purple harvest,
Sayers of the glories of earth and sky,
Of the sweet pain of love
And the keen joy of living;
No longer dreamers of the essential dreams,
And interpreters of the eternal truth,
Through the eternal beauty.
Poets these days are unfortunate fellows.
Baffled in trying to say old things in a new way
Or new things in an old language,
They talk abracadabra
In an unknown tongue,
Each one fashioning for himself

A wordy world of shadow problems,
And as a self-imagined Atlas,
Struggling under it with puny legs and arms,
Groaning out incoherent complaints at his load.

My son, this is no time nor place for a poet;
Grow up and join the big, busy crowd
That scrambles for what it thinks it wants
Out of this old world which is—as it is—
And, probably, always will be.

Take the advice of a father who knows:
You cannot begin too young
Not to be a poet.

Ma Lady's Lips Am Like de Honey

(NEGRO LOVE SONG)

Breeze a-sighin', and a-blowin',
Southern summer night.
Stars a-gleamin' and a-glowin',
Moon jes shinin' right.
Strollin', like all lovers do,
Down de lane wid Lindy Lou;
Honey on her lips to waste;
'Speck I'm gwine to steal a taste.

Oh, ma lady's lips am like de honey,
Ma lady's lips am like de rose;
An' I'm jes like de little bee a-buzzin'
'Round de flower wha' de nectah grows.
Ma lady's lips dey smile so temptin',
Ma lady's teeth so w'ite dey shine,
Oh, ma lady's lips so tantalizin',
Ma lady's lips so close to mine.

Bird a-whistlin' and a-swayin'
In de live-oak tree;
Seems to me he keeps a-sayin',
"Kiss dat gal fo' me!"
Look heah, Mister Mockin' Bird,
Gwine to take you at yo' word;
If I meets ma Waterloo,
Gwine to blame it all on you.

Honey in de rose, I s'pose, is
Put der fo' de bee;
Honey on her lips, I knows, is
Put der jes fo' me.
Seen a sparkle in her eye,
Heard her heave a little sigh;

Felt her kinder squeeze ma han',
'Nuff to make me understan'.

Oh, ma lady's lips am like de honey,
Ma lady's lips am like de rose;
An' I'm jes like de little bee a-buzzin'
'Round de flower wha' de nectah grows.
Ma lady's lips dey smile so temptin',
Ma lady's teeth so w'ite dey shine,
Oh, ma lady's lips so tantalizin',
Ma lady's lips so close to mine.

A Plantation Bacchanal

W'en ole Mister Sun gits tiah'd a-hangin'
High up in de sky;
W'en de rain am a-fallin' an' de thunder am a-bangin',
An' de crap's done all laid by;
W'en yo' bones growin' chilly wid de rheumatics,
Den yo' ride de mule to town,
Git a great big jug o' de ole corn juice,
An' w'en you drink her down—

    Jes lay away ole Trouble,
    An' dry up all yo' tears;
    Yo' pleasure sho' to double
    An' you bound to lose yo' keers.
    Jes lay away ole Sorrer
    High up on de shelf;
    And never mind tomorrer,
    'Twill take care of itself.

W'en ole Mister Age begins a-stealin'
Thoo yo' back an' knees,
W'en yo' bones an' jints lose der limber feelin',
An' am stiff'nin' by degrees;
Now der's jes one way to feel young and spry
W'en you heah dem banjos soun';
Git a great big swig o' de ole corn juice,
An' w'en you drink her down—

    Jes lay away ole Trouble,
    An' dry up all yo' tears;
    Yo' pleasure sho' to double
    An' you bound to lose yo' keers.
    Jes lay away ole Sorrer
    High up on de shelf;
    And never mind tomorrer,
    'Twill take care of itself.

Tunk

(A LECTURE ON EDUCATION BY
A GRANDFATHER)

Look heah, Tunk!—Now, ain't dis awful! T'ought I sont you off
    to school.
Don't you know dat you is growin' up to be a reg'lah fool?

Whah's dem books dat I's done bought you? Look heah, boy,
    you tell me quick,
Whah's dat Webster blue-back spellah an' dat bran' new
    'rifmatic?

W'ile I'm t'inkin' you is lahnin' in de school, why bless ma soul!
You off in de woods a-playin'. Can't you do like you is tole?

Boy, I tell you, it's jes scan'lous d'way dat you is goin' on.
An' you sholy go'n be sorry, jes as true as you is bo'n.

Heah I'm tryin' hard to raise you as a credit to dis race,
An' you tryin' heap much harder fu' to come up in disgrace.

Dese de days w'en men don't git up to de top by hooks an'
    crooks;
Tell you now, dey's got to git der standin' on a pile o' books.

W'en you sees a black man goin' to de fiel' as soon as light,
Followin' a mule across it f'om de mawnin' tel de night,

Wukin' all his life fu' vittles, hoein' 'tween de cott'n rows,
W'en he knocks off ole an' tiah'd, wid nut'n but his ragged
    clo'es,

You kin put it down to ignunce, aftah all what's done an' said,
You kin bet dat dat same black man ain't got nut'n in his head.

Ain't you seed dem w'ite men set'n in der awfice? Don't you
    know
Dey goes der 'bout nine each mawnin'—bless yo' soul, dey's out
    by fo'.

Dey jes does a little writin'; does dat by some easy means;
Gals jes set an' play piannah on dem print'n press muchines.

Chile, dem men knows how to figgah, how to use dat little pen,
An' dey knows dat blue-back spellah f'om beginnin' to de en'.

Dat's de 'fect of education; dat's de t'ing what's gwine to rule;
Git dem books, you lazy rascal! Git back to yo' place in school.

Brer Rabbit, You's de Cutes' of 'Em All

Once der was a meetin' in de wilderness,
All de critters of creation dey was dar;
Brer Rabbit, Brer Possum, Brer Wolf, Brer Fox,
King Lion, Mister Terrapin, Mister B'ar.
De question fu' discussion was, "Who is de bigges' man?"
Dey 'pinted ole Jedge Owl to decide;
He polished up his spectacles an' put 'em on his nose,
An' to the question slowly he replied:

"Brer Wolf am mighty cunnin',
Brer Fox am mighty sly,
Brer Terrapin and Possum—kinder small;
Brer Lion's mighty vicious,
Brer B'ar he's sorter 'spicious,
Brer Rabbit, you's de cutes' of 'em all."

Dis caused a great confusion 'mongst de animals,
Ev'y critter claimed dat he had won de prize;
Dey 'sputed an' dey arg'ed, dey growled an' dey roared,
Den putty soon de dus' begin to rise.
Brer Rabbit he jes' stood aside an' watched 'em w'ile dey fight,
Brer Lion he mos' tore Brer B'ar in two;
W'en dey was all so tiah'd dat dey couldn't catch der bref
Brer Rabbit he jes' grabbed de prize an' flew.

Brer Wolf am mighty cunnin',
Brer Fox am mighty sly,
Brer Terrapin an' Possum—kinder small;
Brer Lion's mighty vicious,
Brer B'ar he's sorter 'spicious,
Brer Rabbit, you's de cutes' of 'em all.

Answer to Prayer

Der ain't no use in sayin' de Lawd won't answer prah;
If you knows how to ax Him, I knows He's bound to heah.

De trouble is, some people don't ax de proper way,
Den w'en dey git's no answer dey doubts de use to pray.

You got to use egzac'ly de 'spressions an' de words
To show dat 'tween yo' faith an' works, you 'pends on works
    two-thirds.

Now, one time I remember—jes how long I won't say—
I thought I'd like a turkey to eat on Chris'mus day

Fu' weeks I dreamed 'bout turkeys, a-strutt'n in der pride;
But seed no way to git one—widout de Lawd pervide.

An' so I went to prayin', I pray'd wid all my might:
"Lawd, sen' *to* me a turkey." I pray'd bofe day an' night.

"Lawd sen' *to* me a turkey, a big one if you please."
I 'clar to heaben I pray'd so much I mos' wore out ma knees.

I pray'd dat prah so often, I pray'd dat prah so long,
Yet didn't git no turkey, I knowed 'twas sump'n wrong.

So on de night 'fore Chris'mus w'en I got down to pray,
"Lawd, sen' *me* to a turkey," I had de sense to say.

"Lawd sen' *me* to a turkey." I know dat prah was right,
An' it was sholy answer'd; I got de bird dat night.

A Banjo Song

W'en de banjos wuz a-ringin',
'N' eyehbody wuz a-singin',
Oh, wuzen dem de good times sho!
All de ole folks would be chattin',
An' de pickaninnies pattin',
As dey heah'd de feet a-shufflin' 'cross de flo'.

An' how we'd dance, an' how we'd sing!
Dance tel de day done break.
An' how dem banjos dey would ring,
An' de cabin flo' would shake!

Come along, come along,
Come along, come along,
Don't you heah dem banjos a-ringin'?

Gib a song, gib a song,
Gib a song, gib a song,
Git yo' feet fixed up fu' a-wingin'.

W'ile de banjos dey go plunka-plunka-plunk,
We'll dance tel de ole flo' shake;
W'ile de feet keep a-goin' chooka-chooka-chook,
We'll dance tel de day done break.

The Rivals

Look heah! Is I evah tole you 'bout de curious way I won
Anna Liza? Say, I nevah? Well heah's how de thing wuz done.

Lize, you know, wuz mighty purty—dat's been forty
    yeahs ago—
'N' 'cos to look at her dis minit, you might'n s'pose dat it
    wuz so.

She wuz jes de greates' 'traction in de country, 'n' bless de Lam'!
Eveh lovin' man wuz co'tin', but it lay 'twix me an' Sam.

You know Sam. We both wuz wu'kin' on de ole John
    Tompkin's place.
'N' evehbody wuz a-watchin' t'see who's gwine to win de race.

Hee! hee! hee! Now you mus' raley 'scuse me fu' dis snickering,
But I jes can't he'p f'om laffin' eveh time I tells dis thing.

Ez I wuz a-sayin', me an' Sam wu'ked daily side by side,
He a-studyin', me a-studyin' how to win Lize fu' a bride.

Well, de race wuz kinder equal, Lize wuz sorter on de fence;
Sam he had de mostes dollars, an' I had de mostes sense.

Things dey run along 'bout eben tel der come Big Meetin' day;
Sam den thought, to win Miss Liza, he had foun' de shoest way.

An' you talk about big meetin's! None been like it 'fore nor
    sence;
Der wuz sich a crowd o' people dat we had to put up tents.

Der wuz preachers f'om de Eas', an' der wuz preachers f'om
    de Wes';
Folks had kilt mos' eveh chicken, an wuz fattenin' up de res'.

Gals had all got new w'ite dresses, an' bought ribbens fu' der
    hair,
Fixin' fu' de openin' Sunday, prayin' dat de day'd be fair.

Dat de Reveren' Jasper Jones of Mount Moriah, it wuz 'llowed,
Wuz to preach de openin' sermon; so you know der wuz a
    crowd.

Fu' dat man wuz sho' a preacher; had a voice jes like a bull;
So der ain't no use in sayin' dat de meetin' house wuz full.

Folks wuz der f'om Big Pine Hollow, some come 'way f'om
    Muddy Creek,
Some come jes to stay fu' Sunday, but de crowd stay'd thoo de
    week.

Some come ridin' in top-buggies wid de w'eels all painted red,
Pulled by mules dat run like rabbits, each one tryin' to git ahead.

Othah po'rer folks come drivin' mules dat leaned up 'ginst de
    shaf',
Hitched to broke-down, creaky wagons dat looked like dey'd
    drap in half.

But de bigges' crowd come walkin', wid der new shoes on der
    backs;
'Scuse wuz dat dey couldn't weah em 'cause de heels wuz full o'
    tacks.

Fact is, it's a job for Job, a-trudgin' in de sun an' heat,
Down a long an' dusty clay road wid yo' shoes packed full o'
    feet.

'Cose dey stopt an' put dem shoes on w'en dey got mos' to
    de do';
Den dey had to grin an' bear it; dat tuk good religion sho.

But I mos' forgot ma story—well at las' dat Sunday came
And it seemed dat evehbody, blin' an' deef, an' halt an' lame

Wuz out in de grove a-waitin' fu' de meetin' to begin;
Ef dat crowd had got converted 'twould a been de end o' sin.

Lize wuz der in all her glory, purty ez a big sunflowah.
I kin 'member how she looked jes same ez 'twuz dis ve'y houah.

But to make my story shorter, w'ile we wuz a-waitin' der,
Down de road we spied a cloud o' dus' dat filled up all de air.

An' ez we kep' on a-lookin', out f'om 'mongst dat ve'y cloud,
Sam, on Marse John's big mule, Cæsar, rode right slam up in de
    crowd.

You jes oughtah seed dat feller, 'clar I like tah los' ma bref;
Fu' to use a common 'spression, he wuz 'bout nigh dressed
    to def.

He had slipped to town dat Sat'day, didn't let nobody know,
An' had carried all his cash an' lef' it in de dry-goods sto'.

He had on a bran' new suit o' sto'-bought clo'es, a high
    plug hat;
He looked 'zactly like a gen'man, 'tain't no use d'nyin' dat.

W'en he got down off dat mule an' bowed to Liza I could see
How she looked at him so 'dmirin', an' jes kinder glanced at me.

Den I know'd to win dat gal, I sho' would need some othah
    means
'Sides a-hangin' 'round big meetin' in a suit o' homespun jeans.

W'en dey blowed de ho'n fu' preachin', an' de crowd all went
    inside,
I jes felt ez doh I'd like tah go off in de woods an' hide.

So I stay'd outside de meetin', set'n underneat' de trees,
Seemed to me I sot der ages, wid ma elbows on ma knees.

W'en dey sung dat hymn, "Nobody knows de trouble dat I see,"
Seem'd to me dat dey wuz singin' eveh word o' it fu' me.

Jes how long I might ha' sot der, actin' like a cussed fool,
I don't know, but it jes happen'd dat I look'd an' saw Sam's
    mule,

An' de thought come slowly tricklin' thoo ma brain right der
    an' den,
Dat, perhaps, wid some persuasion, I could make dat mule ma
    fren'.

An' I jes kep' on a-thinkin', an' I kep' a-lookin' 'roun',
Tel I spied two great big san' spurs right close by me on de
    groun'.

Well, I took dem spurs an' put em underneat' o' Cæsar's saddle,
So dey'd press down in his backbone soon ez Sam had got
    a-straddle.

'Twuz a pretty ticklish job, an' jes ez soon ez it wuz done,
I went back w'ere I wuz set'n fu' to wait an' see de fun.

Purty soon heah come de people, jes a-swa'min' out de do',
Talkin' 'bout de "pow'ful sermon"—"nevah heah'd de likes
    befo'."

How de "monahs fell convicted" jes de same ez lumps o' lead,
How dat some wuz still a-layin' same ez if dey'd been struck
    dead.

An' to rectly heah come Liza, Sam a-strollin' by her side,
An' it seem'd to me his smile wuz jest about twelve inches wide.

Look to me like he had swelled up to 'bout twice his natchul
     size,
An' I heah'd him say, "I'd like to be yo' 'scort tonight, Miss
     Lize."

Den he made a bow jes like he's gwine to make a speech in
     school,
An' walk'd off ez proud ez Marse John, over to ontie his mule,

W'en Sam's foot fust touched de stirrup he know'd der wuz
     sump'n wrong;
'Cuz de mule begin to tremble an' to sorter side along.

W'en Sam raised his weight to mount him, Cæsar bristled up
     his ear,
W'en Sam sot down in de saddle, den dat mule commenced to
     rear.

An' he reared an' pitched an' caper'd, only ez a mule kin pitch,
Tel he flung Sam clean f'om off him, landed him squar' in a
     ditch.

W'en Sam riz up, well, I tell you, I felt kinder bad fu' him;
He had bust dem cheap sto' britches f'om de center to de rim.

All de plug hat dat wuz lef' him wuz de brim aroun' his neck,
Smear'd wid mud f'om top to bottom—well, he wuz a sight, I
     'speck.

Wuz de folks a-laffin'? Well su', I jes sholy thought dey'd bus'.
Wuz Sam laffin'? 'Twuz de fus' time dat I evah heah'd him cuss.

W'ile Sam slink'd off thoo de back woods I walk'd slowly home
     wid Lize.
W'en I axed her jes one question der wuz sump'n in her eyes

Made me know der wuz no need o' any answer bein' said,
An' I felt jes like de whole world wuz a-spinnin' roun' ma head.

So I said, "Lize, w'en we marry, mus' I weah some sto'-bought
  clo'es?"

She says, "Jeans is good enough fu' any po' folks, heaben
  knows!"

Sence You Went Away

Seems lak to me de stars don't shine so bright,
Seems lak to me de sun done loss his light,
Seems lak to me der's nothin' goin' right,
   Sence you went away.

Seems lak to me de sky ain't half so blue,
Seems lak to me dat ev'ything wants you,
Seems lak to me I don't know what to do,
   Sence you went away.

Seems lak to me dat ev'ything is wrong,
Seems lak to me de day's jes twice ez long,
Seems lak to me de bird's forgot his song,
   Sence you went away.

Seems lak to me I jes can't he'p but sigh,
Seems lak to me ma th'oat keeps gittin' dry,
Seems lak to me a tear stays in ma eye,
   Sence you went away.

Lift Every Voice and Sing

A group of young men in Jacksonville, Florida, arranged to celebrate Lincoln's birthday in 1900. My brother, J. Rosamond Johnson, and I decided to write a song to be sung at the exercises. I wrote the words and he wrote the music. Our New York publisher, Edward B. Marks, made mimeographed copies for us, and the song was taught to and sung by a chorus of five hundred colored school children.

Shortly afterwards my brother and I moved away from Jacksonville to New York, and the song passed out of our minds. But the school children of Jacksonville kept singing it; they went off to other schools and sang it; they became teachers and taught it to other children. Within twenty years it was being sung over the South and in some other parts of the country. Today the song, popularly known as the Negro National Hymn, is quite generally used.

The lines of this song repay me in an elation, almost of exquisite anguish, whenever I hear them sung by Negro children.

Lift every voice and sing
Till earth and heaven ring,
Ring with the harmonies of Liberty;
Let our rejoicing rise
High as the listening skies,
Let it resound loud as the rolling sea.
Sing a song full of the faith that the dark past has taught us,
Sing a song full of the hope that the present has brought us.
Facing the rising sun of our new day begun,
Let us march on till victory is won.

Stony the road we trod,
Bitter the chastening rod,
Felt in the days when hope unborn had died;
Yet with a steady beat,

Have not our weary feet
Come to the place for which our fathers sighed?
We have come over a way that with tears has been watered,
We have come, treading our path through the blood of the
    slaughtered,
Out from the gloomy past,
Till now we stand at last
Where the white gleam of our bright star is cast.

God of our weary years,
God of our silent tears,
Thou who hast brought us thus far on the way;
Thou who hast by Thy might
Led us into the light,
Keep us forever in the path, we pray.
Lest our feet stray from the places, our God, where we met
    Thee,
Lest, our hearts drunk with the wine of the world, we forget
    Thee;
Shadowed beneath Thy hand,
May we forever stand.
True to our God,
True to our native land.

Envoy

If homely virtues draw from me a tune
In jingling rhyme—or in ambitious rune;
Or if the smoldering future should inspire
My hand to try the seer's prophetic lyre;
Or if injustice, brutishness, and wrong
Stir me to make a weapon of my song;

O God, give beauty, truth, strength to my words—
Oh, may they fall like sweetly cadenced chords,
Or burn like beacon fires from out the dark,
Or speed like arrows, swift and sure to the mark.

FIFTY YEARS AND OTHER POEMS *was first published in 1917. The bulk of the poems in* Fifty Years *were republished in* Saint Peter Relates an Incident *in 1935, and the remainder of the poems are included here, along with the 1917 introduction by James Weldon Johnson's literary mentor, Columbia University's Brander Matthews.*

Introduction by Brander Matthews

Of the hundred millions who make up the population of the United States ten millions come from a stock ethnically alien to the other ninety millions. They are not descended from ancestors who came here voluntarily, in the spirit of adventure to better themselves or in the spirit of devotion to make sure of freedom to worship God in their own way. They are the grandchildren of men and women brought here against their wills to serve as slaves. It is only half-a-century since they received their freedom and since they were at last permitted to own themselves. They are now American citizens, with the rights and the duties of other American citizens; and they know no language, no literature and no law other than those of their fellow citizens of Anglo-Saxon ancestry.

When we take stock of ourselves these ten millions cannot be left out of account. Yet they are not as we are; they stand apart, more or less; they have their own distinct characteristics. It behooves us to understand them as best we can and to discover what manner of people they are. And we are justified in inquiring how far they have revealed themselves, their racial characteristics, their abiding traits, their longing aspirations—how far have they disclosed these in one or another of the several arts. They have had their poets, their painters, their composers, and yet most of these have ignored their racial opportunity and have worked in imitation and in emulation of their white predecessors and contemporaries, content to handle again the traditional themes. The most important and the most significant contributions they have made to art are in music,—first in the plaintive beauty of the so-called "Negro spirituals"—and, secondly, in the syncopated melody of so-called "rag-time" which has now taken the whole world captive.

In poetry, especially in the lyric, wherein the soul is free to find full expression for its innermost emotions, their attempts have been, for the most part, divisible into two classes. In the first of these may be grouped the verses in which the lyrist put forth sentiments common to all mankind and in no wise specifically those of his own race; and from the days of Phillis Wheatley to the present the most of the poems written by men who were not wholly white are indistinguishable from the poems written by men who were wholly white. Whatever their merits might be, these verses cast little or no light upon the deeper racial sentiments of the people to whom the poets themselves belonged. But in the lyrics to be grouped in the second of these classes there was a racial quality. This contained the dialect verses in which there was an avowed purpose of recapturing the color, the flavor, the movement of life in "the quarters," in the cotton field and in the canebrake. Even in this effort, white authors had led the way; Irvin Russell and Joel Chandler Harris had made the path straight for Paul Laurence Dunbar, with his lilting lyrics, often infused with the pathos of a down-trodden folk.

In the following pages Mr. James Weldon Johnson conforms to both of these traditions. He gathers together a group of lyrics, delicate in workmanship, fragrant with sentiment, and phrased in pure and unexceptionable English. Then he has another group of dialect verses, racy of the soil, pungent in flavor, swinging in rhythm and adroit in rhyme. But where he shows himself a pioneer is the half-dozen larger and bolder poems, of a loftier strain, in which he has been nobly successful in expressing the higher aspirations of his own people. It is in uttering this cry for recognition, for sympathy, for understanding, and above all, for justice, that Mr. Johnson is most original and most powerful. In the superb and soaring stanzas of "Fifty Years" (published exactly half-a-century after the signing of the Emancipation Proclamation) he has given us one of the noblest commemorative poems yet written by any American,—a poem sonorous in its diction, vigorous in its workmanship, elevated in its imagination and sincere in its emotion. In it speaks the voice of his race; and the race is fortunate in its spokesman. In it a fine theme has been finely treated. In it we are made to see something of the soul of the people who are our fellow citizens now and forever,—even if we do not always so regard them. In it we are glad to acclaim a poem which any living poet might be proud to call his own.

Fifty Years
(1863–1913)

I had for some while been revolving in my mind the idea of writing a poem in commemoration of the fiftieth anniversary of the signing of the Emancipation Proclamation. Because of some mental quirk I kept thinking that that anniversary would fall in 1915. In the early part of October, 1912, I learned that the fiftieth anniversary of the preliminary proclamation, which Lincoln signed September 22, 1862, was being celebrated; and I realized that I had, instead of a little more than two years, only a little more than two months in which to do the poem. I was at the time on consular duty in Nicaragua, and in the midst of the beginning of the American military occupation of that country. The consulate had been made Marine headquarters, there was constant coming and going of officers and troops; machine-guns were mounted in front of the house, and at night a hundred or more Marines slept in the *patio*. I found it possible to write only after midnight.

I finished the poem in the first part of December and sent it to my friend, Brander Matthews, at Columbia University. Professor Matthews sent it to the *New York Times*, and it was published in that newspaper on January 1, 1913, the precise date of the fiftieth anniversary.

As first written, the poem consisted of forty-one stanzas. At the point where it reached its highest expression of achievement and of faith in the realization of well-earned rights, it took a turn and brought into view the other side of the shield, and ended on a note of bitterness and despair. I saw that the last part of the composition, though voicing the verities, nullified the theme, purpose, and effect of the poem as a whole. After a struggle in which my better taste and judgment won, I cut off the last stanzas.

O brothers mine, today we stand
　　Where half a century sweeps our ken,
Since God, through Lincoln's ready hand,
　　Struck off our bonds and made us men.

Just fifty years—a winter's day,
　　As runs the history of a race;
Yet, as we look back o'er the way,
　　How distant seems our starting place!

Look farther back! Three centuries!
　　To where a naked, shivering score,
Snatched from their haunts across the seas,
　　Stood, wide-eyed, on Virginia's shore.

Then let us here erect a stone,
　　To mark the place, to mark the time;
As witness to God's purpose shown,
　　A pledge to hold this day sublime.

A part of His unknown design,
　　We've lived within a mighty age;
And we have helped to write a line
　　On history's most wondrous page.

A few black bondmen strewn along
　　The borders of our eastern coast,
Now grown a race, ten million strong,
　　An upward, onward, marching host.

Far, far the way that we have trod,
　　From slave and pagan denizens,
To freedmen, freemen, sons of God,
　　Americans and Citizens.

For never let the thought arise
　　That we are here on sufferance bare;

Outcasts asylumed 'neath these skies,
  And aliens without part or share.

This land is ours by right of birth,
  This land is ours by right of toil;
We helped to turn its virgin earth,
  Our sweat is in its fruitful soil.

Where once the tangled forest stood,
  Where flourished once rank weed and thorn,
Behold the path-traced, peaceful wood,
  The cotton white, the yellow corn.

To gain these fruits that have been earned,
  To hold these fields that have been won,
Our arms have strained, our backs have burned,
  Bent bare beneath a ruthless sun.

That Banner which is now the type
  Of victory on field and flood—
Remember, its first crimson stripe
  Was dyed by Attucks' willing blood.

And never yet has come the cry—
  When that fair flag has been assailed—
For men to do, for men to die,
  That we have faltered or have failed.

We've helped to bear it, rent and torn,
  Through many a hot-breath'd battle breeze;
Held in our hands, it has been borne
  And planted far across the seas.

And never yet—O haughty Land,
  Let us, at least, for this be praised—
Has one black, treason-guided hand
  Ever against that flag been raised.

Then should we speak but servile words,
    Or shall we hang our heads in shame?
Stand back of new-come foreign hordes,
    And fear our heritage to claim?

No! Stand erect and without fear,
    And for our foes let this suffice—
We've brought a rightful sonship here,
    And we have more than paid the price.

And yet, my brothers, well I know
    The tethered feet, the pinioned wings,
The spirit bowed beneath the blow,
    The heart grown faint from wounds and stings;

The staggering force of brutish might,
    That strikes and leaves us stunned and dazed;
The long, vain waiting through the night
    To hear some voice for justice raised.

Full well I know the hour when hope
    Sinks dead, and round us everywhere
Hangs stifling darkness, and we grope
    With hands uplifted in despair.

Courage! Look out, beyond, and see
    The far horizon's beckoning span!
Faith in your God-known destiny!
    We are a part of some great plan.

Because the tongues of Garrison
    And Phillips now are cold in death,
Think you their work can be undone?
    Or quenched the fires lit by their breath?

Think you that John Brown's spirit stops?
    That Lovejoy was but idly slain?

Or do you think those precious drops
  From Lincoln's heart were shed in vain?

That for which millions prayed and sighed,
  That for which tens of thousands fought,
For which so many freely died,
  God cannot let it come to naught.

To Horace Bumstead

Have you been sore discouraged in the fight,
   And even sometimes weighted by the thought
   That those with whom and those for whom you fought
Lagged far behind, or dared but faintly smite?
And that the opposing forces in their might
   Of blind inertia rendered as for naught
   All that throughout the long years had been wrought,
And powerless each blow for Truth and Right?

If so, take new and greater courage then,
   And think no more withouten help you stand;
    For sure as God on His eternal throne
Sits, mindful of the sinful deeds of men,
   —The awful Sword of Justice in His hand,—
    You shall not, no, you shall not, fight alone.

The Color Sergeant

(ON AN INCIDENT AT THE
BATTLE OF SAN JUAN HILL)

Under a burning tropic sun,
With comrades around him lying,
A trooper of the sable Tenth
Lay wounded, bleeding, dying.

First in the charge up the fort-crowned hill,
His company's guidon bearing,
He had rushed where the leaden hail fell fast,
Not death nor danger fearing.

He fell in the front where the fight grew fierce,
Still faithful in life's last labor;
Black though his skin, yet his heart as true
As the steel of his blood-stained saber.

And while the battle around him rolled,
Like the roar of a sullen breaker.
He closed his eyes on the bloody scene,
And presented arms to his Maker.

There he lay, without honor or rank,
But, still, in a grim-like beauty;
Despised of men for his humble race,
Yet true, in death, to his duty.

From the German of Uhland

Three students once tarried over the Rhine,
And into Frau Wirthin's turned to dine.

"Say, hostess, have you good beer and wine?
And where is that pretty daughter of thine?"

"My beer and wine is fresh and clear.
My daughter lies on her funeral bier."

They softly tipped into the room;
She lay there in the silent gloom.

The first the white cloth gently raised,
And tearfully upon her gazed.

"If thou wert alive, O, lovely maid,
My heart at thy feet would to-day be laid!"

The second covered her face again,
And turned away with grief and pain.

"Ah, thou upon thy snow-white bier!
And I have loved thee so many a year."

The third drew back again the veil,
And kissed the lips so cold and pale.

"I've loved thee always, I love thee to-day,
And will love thee, yes, forever and aye!"

Before a Painting

I knew not who had wrought with skill so fine
   What I beheld; nor by what laws of art
   He had created life and love and heart
On canvas, from mere color, curve and line.
Silent I stood and made no move or sign;
   Not with the crowd, but reverently apart;
   Nor felt the power my rooted limbs to start,
But mutely gazed upon that face divine.

And over me the sense of beauty fell,
   As music over a raptured listener to
      The deep-voiced organ breathing out a hymn;
Or as on one who kneels, his beads to tell,
   There falls the aureate glory filtered through
      The windows in some old cathedral dim.

I Hear the Stars Still Singing

I hear the stars still singing
To the beautiful, silent night,
As they speed with noiseless winging
Their ever westward flight,
I hear the waves still falling
On the stretch of lonely shore,
But the sound of a sweet voice calling
I shall hear, alas! no more.

A Mid-Day Dreamer

I love to sit alone, and dream,
And dream, and dream;
In fancy's boat to softly glide
Along some stream
Where fairy palaces of gold
And crystal bright
Stand all along the glistening shore:
A wondrous sight.

My craft is built of ivory,
With silver oars,
The sails are spun of golden threads,
And priceless stores
Of precious gems adorn its prow,
And 'round its mast
An hundred silken cords are set
To hold it fast.

My galley-slaves are sprightly elves
Who, as they row,
And as their shining oars they swing
Them to and fro,
Keep time to music wafted on
The scented air,
Made by the mermaids as they comb
Their golden hair.

And I the while lie idly back,
And dream, and dream,
And let them row me where they will
Adown the stream.

The Temptress

Old Devil, when you come with horns and tail,
With diabolic grin and crafty leer;
I say, such bogey-man devices wholly fail
To waken in my heart a single fear.

But when you wear a form I know so well,
A form so human, yet so near divine;
'Tis then I fall beneath the magic of your spell,
'Tis then I know the vantage is not mine.

Ah! when you take your horns from off your head,
And soft and fragrant hair is in their place;
I must admit I fear the tangled path I tread
When that dear head is laid against my face.

And at what time you change your baleful eyes
For stars that melt into the gloom of night,
All of my courage, my dear fellow, quickly flies;
I know my chance is slim to win the fight.

And when, instead of charging down to wreck
Me on a red-hot pitchfork in your hand,
You throw a pair of slender arms about my neck,
I dare not trust the ground on which I stand.

Whene'er in place of using patent wile,
Or trying to frighten me with horrid grin,
You tempt me with two crimson lips curved in a smile;
Old Devil, I must really own, you win.

The Ghost of Deacon Brown

In a backwoods town
Lived Deacon Brown,
And he was a miser old;
He would trust no bank,
So he dug, and sank
In the ground a box of gold,
Down deep in the ground a box of gold.

He hid his gold,
As has been told,
He remembered that he did it;
But sad to say,
On the very next day,
He forgot just where he hid it:
To find his gold he tried and tried
Till he grew faint and sick, and died.

Then on each dark and gloomy night
A form in phosphorescent white,
A genuine hair-raising sight,
Would wander through the town.
And as it slowly roamed around,
With a spade it dug each foot of ground;
So the folks about
Said there was no doubt
'Twas the ghost of Deacon Brown.

Around the church
This Ghost would search,
And whenever it would see
The passers-by
Take wings and fly
It would laugh in ghostly glee
Hee, hee!—it would laugh in ghostly glee.

And so the town
Went quickly down,
For they said that it was haunted;
And doors and gates,
So the story states,
Bore a notice, "Tenants wanted."

And the town is now for let,
But the ghost is digging yet.

"Lazy"

Some men enjoy the constant strife
Of days with work and worry rife,
But that is not my dream of life:
   I think such men are crazy.
For me, a life with worries few,
A job of nothing much to do,
Just pelf enough to see me through:
   I fear that I am lazy.

On winter mornings cold and drear,
When six o'clock alarms I hear,
'Tis then I love to shift my ear,
   And hug my downy pillows.
When in the shade it's ninety-three,
No job in town looks good to me,
I'd rather loaf down by the sea,
   And watch the foaming billows.

Some people think the world's a school,
Where labor is the only rule;
But I'll not make myself a mule,
   And don't you ever doubt it.
I know that work may have its use,
But still I feel that's no excuse
For turning it into abuse;
   What do *you* think about it?

Let others fume and sweat and boil,
And scratch and dig for golden spoil,
And live the life of work and toil,
   Their lives to labor giving.
But what is gold when life is sped,
And life is short, as has been said,
And we are such a long time dead,
   I'll spend my life in living.

Omar

Old Omar, jolly sceptic, it may be
That, after all, you found the magic key
To life and all its mystery, and I
Must own you have almost persuaded me.

Voluptas (I)

To chase a never-reached mirage
Across the hot, white sand,
And choke and die, while gazing on
Its green and watered strand.

The Word of an Engineer

"She's built of steel
From deck to keel,
And bolted strong and tight;
In scorn she'll sail
The fiercest gale,
And pierce the darkest night.

"The builder's art
Has proved each part
Throughout her breadth and length;
Deep in the hulk,
Of her mighty bulk,
Ten thousand Titans' strength."

The tempest howls,
The Ice Wolf prowls,
The winds they shift and veer,
But calm I sleep,
And faith I keep
In the word of an engineer.

Along the trail
Of the slender rail
The train, like a nightmare, flies
And dashes on
Through the black-mouthed yawn
Where the cavernous tunnel lies.

Over the ridge,
Across the bridge,
Swung twixt the sky and hell,
On an iron thread
Spun from the head
Of the man in a draughtsman's cell.

And so we ride
Over land and tide,
Without a thought of fear—
Man never had
The faith in God
That he has in an engineer!

The Gift to Sing

Sometimes the mist overhangs my path,
And blackening clouds about me cling;
But, oh, I have a magic way
To turn the gloom to cheerful day—
    I softly sing.

And if the way grows darker still,
Shadowed by Sorrow's somber wing,
With glad defiance in my throat,
I pierce the darkness with a note,
    And sing, and sing.

I brood not over the broken past,
Nor dread whatever time may bring;
No nights are dark, no days are long,
While in my heart there swells a song,
    And I can sing.

Morning, Noon and Night

When morning shows her first faint flush,
I think of the tender blush
That crept so gently to your cheek
When first my love I dared to speak;
How, in your glance, a dawning ray
Gave promise of love's perfect day.

When, in the ardent breath of noon,
The roses with passion swoon;
There steals upon me from the air
The scent that lurked within your hair;
I touch your hand, I clasp your form—
Again your lips are close and warm.

When comes the night with beauteous skies,
I think of your tear-dimmed eyes,
Their mute entreaty that I stay,
Although your lips sent me away;
And then falls memory's bitter blight,
And dark—so dark becomes the night.

The Awakening

I dreamed that I was a rose
That grew beside a lonely way,
Close by a path none ever chose,
And there I lingered day by day.
Beneath the sunshine and the show'r
I grew and waited there apart,
Gathering perfume hour by hour,
And storing it within my heart,
   Yet, never knew,
Just why I waited there and grew.

I dreamed that you were a bee
That one day gaily flew along,
You came across the hedge to me,
And sang a soft, love-burdened song.
You brushed my petals with a kiss,
I woke to gladness with a start,
And yielded up to you in bliss
The treasured fragrance of my heart;
   And then I knew
That I had waited there for you.

Venus in a Garden

'Twas at early morning,
The dawn was blushing in her purple bed,
When in a sweet, embowered garden
She, the fairest of the goddesses,
The lovely Venus,
Roamed amongst the roses white and red.
She sought for flowers
To make a garland
For her golden head.

Snow-white roses, blood-red roses,
In that sweet garden close,
Offered incense to the goddess:
Both the white and the crimson rose.

White roses, red roses, blossoming:
But the fair Venus knew
The crimson roses had gained their hue
From the hearts that for love had bled;
And the goddess made a garland
Gathered from the roses red.

Nobody's Lookin' But de Owl and de Moon
(A NEGRO SERENADE)

De river is a-glistenin' in de moonlight,
De owl is set'n high up in de tree;
De little stars am twinklin' wid a sof' light,
De night seems only jes fu' you an' me.
Thoo de trees de breezes am a-sighin',
Breathin' out a sort o' lover's croon,
Der's nobody lookin' or a-spyin',
Nobody but de owl an' de moon.

Nobody's lookin' but de owl an' de moon,
An' de night is balmy; fu' de month is June;
Come den, Honey, won't you? Come to meet me soon,
W'ile nobody's lookin' but de owl an' de moon.

I feel so kinder lonely all de daytime,
It seems I raly don't know what to do;
I jes keep sort a-longin' fu' de night-time,
'Cause den I know dat I can be wid you.
An' de thought jes sets my brain a-swayin',
An' my heart a-beatin' to a tune;
Come, de owl won't tell w'at we's a-sayin',
An' cose you know we kin trus' de moon.

You's Sweet to Yo' Mammy Jes de Same

(LULLABY)

Shet yo' eyes, ma little pickaninny, go to sleep
Mammy's watchin' by you all de w'ile;
Daddy is a-wukin' down in de cott'n fiel',
Wukin' fu' his little honey child.
An' yo' mammy's heart is jes a-brimmin' full o'lub
Fu' you f'om yo' head down to yo' feet;
Oh, no mattah w'at some othah folks may t'ink o' you,
To yo' mammy's heart you's mighty sweet.

You's sweet to yo' mammy jes de same;
Dat's why she calls you Honey fu' yo' name.
Yo' face is black, dat's true,
An' yo' hair is woolly, too,
But, you's sweet to yo' mammy jes de same.

Up der in de big house w'ere dey lib so rich an' gran'
Dey's got chillen dat dey lubs, I s'pose;
Chillen dat is purty, oh, but dey can't lub dem mo'
Dan yo' mammy lubs you, heaben knows!

Dey may t'ink you's homely, an' yo' clo'es dey may be po',
But yo' shinin' eyes, dey hol's a light
Dat, my Honey, w'en you opens dem so big an' roun',
Makes you lubly in yo' mammy's sight.

July in Georgy

I'm back down in ole Georgy w'ere de sun is shinin' hot,
W'ere de cawn it is a-tasslin', gittin' ready fu' de pot;

W'ere de cott'n is a-openin' an' a-w'itenin' in de sun,
An' de ripenin' o' de sugah-cane is mighty nigh begun.

An' de locus' is a-singin' f'om eveh bush an' tree,
An' you kin heah de hummin' o' de noisy bumblebee;

An' de mule he stan's a-dreamin' an' a-dreamin' in de lot,
An' de sun it is a-shinin' mighty hot, hot, hot.

But evehbody is a-restin', fu' de craps is all laid by,
An' time fu' de camp-meetin' is a drawin' purty nigh;

An' we's put away de ploughshare, an' we's done hung up de
    spade,
An' we's eatin' watermelon, an' a-layin' in de shade.

Dat Gal o' Mine

Skin as black an' jes as sof' as a velvet dress,
Teeth as white as ivory—well dey is I guess.

Eyes dat's jes as big an' bright as de evenin' star;
An' dat hol' some sort o' light lublier by far.

Hair don't hang 'way down her back; plaited up in rows;
Wid de two en's dat's behin' tied wid ribben bows.

Han's dat raly wuz'n made fu' hard work, I'm sho';
Got a little bit o' foot; weahs a numbah fo'.

You jes oughtah see dat gal Sunday's w'en she goes
To de Baptis' meetin' house, dressed in her bes' clo'es.

W'en she puts her w'ite dress on an' othah things so fine;
Now, Su', don't you know I'm proud o' dat gal o' mine.

The Seasons

W'en de leaves begin to fall,
An' de fros' is on de ground,
An' de 'simmons is a-ripenin' on de tree;
W'en I heah de dinner call,
An' de chillen gadder 'round,
'Tis den de 'possum is de meat fu' me.

W'en de wintertime am pas'
An' de spring is come at las',
W'en de good ole summer sun begins to shine;
Oh! my thoughts den tek a turn,
An' my heart begins to yearn
Fo' dat watermelon growin' on de vine.

Now, de yeah will sholy bring
'Round a season fu' us all,
Ev'y one kin pick his season f'om de res';
But de melon in de spring,
An' de 'possum in de fall,
Mek it hard to tell which time o' year am bes'.

'Possum Song
(A WARNING)

'Simmons ripenin' in de fall,
You better run,
Brudder 'Possum, run!
Mockin' bird commence to call,
You better run, Brudder 'Possum, git out de way!
You better run, Brudder 'Possum, git out de way!
Run some whar an' hide!
Ole moon am sinkin'
Down behin' de tree.
Ole Eph am thinkin'
An' chuckelin' wid glee.
Ole Tige am blinkin'
An' frisky as kin be,
Yo' chances, Brudder 'Possum,
Look mighty slim to me.

Run, run, run, I tell you,
Run, Brudder 'Possum, run!
Run, run, run, I tell you,
Ole Eph's got a gun.
Pickaninnies grinnin'
Waitin' fu' to see de fun.
You better run, Brudder 'Possum, git out de way!
Run, Brudder 'Possum, run!

Brudder 'Possum take a tip;
You better run,
Brudder 'Possum, run!
'Tain't no use in actin' flip,
You better run, Brudder 'Possum, git out de way!
You better run, Brudder 'Possum, git out de way!
Run some whar an' hide.
Dey's gwine to houn' you
All along de line,

W'en dey done foun' you,
Den what's de use in sighin'?
Wid taters roun' you,
You sholy would tase fine—
So listen, Brudder 'Possum,
You better be a-flyin'.

Run, run, run, I tell you,
Run, Brudder 'Possum, run!
Run, run, run, I tell you,
Ole Eph's got a gun.
Pickaninnies grinnin'
Waitin' fu' to see de fun.
You better run, Brudder 'Possum, git out de way!
Run, Brudder 'Possum, run!

An Explanation

Look heah! 'Splain to me de reason
Why you said to Squire Lee,
Der wuz twelve ole chicken thieves
In dis heah town, includin' me.
Ef he tole you dat, my brudder,
He said sump'n dat warn't true;
W'at I said wuz dis, dat der wuz
Twelve, *widout* includin' you.

Oh! . . . !—

De Little Pickaninny's Gone to Sleep

Cuddle down, ma honey, in yo' bed,
Go to sleep an' res' yo' little head,
Been a-kind o' ailin' all de day?
Didn't have no sperit fu' to play?
Never min', to-morrer, w'en you wek,
Daddy's gwine to ride you on his bek,
'Roun' an' roun' de cabin flo' so fas'—
Der! He's closed his little eyes at las'.

De little pickaninny's gone to sleep,
Cuddled in his trundle bed so tiny,
De little pickaninny's gone to sleep,
Closed his little eyes so bright an' shiny.
Hush! an' w'en you walk across de flo'
Step across it very sof' an' slow.
De shadders all aroun' begin to creep,
De little pickaninny's gone to sleep.

Mandy, w'at's de matter wid dat chile?
Keeps a-sighin' ev'y little w'ile;
Seems to me I heayhd him sorter groan,
Lord! his little han's am col' as stone!
W'at's dat far-off light dat's in his eyes?
Dat's a light dey's borrow'd f'om de skies;
Fol' his little han's across his breas',
Let de little pickaninny res'.

PART III

College Years and Other Poems

THE BULK OF *the following poems were written during James Weldon Johnson's years as a college student at Atlanta University (1890–94). The poems "Moods," "A Passing Melody," "The River," and "Helene," however, were written during the early part of the twentieth century. His college poems presented here are imitative of well-known English poets whom he had studied as an undergraduate student. These poems, however, shed light on his creativity in its early stages without detracting from his interest in the traditions, folklore, and struggles of African Americans that is so clearly evident in his later work. Moreover, these poems document the emergence and growth of Johnson as a poet. The majority of this selection are published here for the first time.*

Moods

I love the sea when it is windswept
The ships ploughing up the foam,
The sailor man loudly swearing
From sheer excess of joy,
The shrill cry of a solitary sea bird,
And the smell of the sharp, salt spray.

I love the melancholy beach
Under the shimmering magic of the moon.
When just above the ocean's rim
One lone star marks a path for me;
And the waves are moaning to the shore
Their monotoned love melody.

A Passing Melody

A chord was touched on the harp of my heart,
On the delicate strings at the core;
A tender, hesitating part
I had never heard before.

It quivered there one moment brief,
Awakening hopes and fears,
Imparting joy, suggesting grief,
Then melted into tears.

Oh! was it a long lost love that cleaves
To the dead, forgotten past?
Or but the rustling of the leaves,
Stirred by the winter's blast?

The River

When the earth was young this river
Was a thing of unsoiled beauty.
It gurgled down from the hill,
And hymned its way through the valley.
A pageant in the sunlight,
A mystery under the moon,
And a symbol of all eternity
Where it lost itself in the ocean.

I crossed the river the other day
On a hideous ferryboat,
I leaned on the rail and watched the wheel
Savagely churn up the water.
It churned up time and boxes,
Jute bags and rotten cabbages,
A cat some seven days drowned
And a stench that went to the stomach.

The river hissed and frothed
In piteous indignation.
I thought: Why this hissing and frothing,
Do you not know
That the ultimate end of all beautiful rivers
Is to carry sewage to the sea?

Helene

I walk by day, I wake by night,
Thirsting, panting for your beauty—
And ever, ever at my side
There stalks a spectre men call Duty.

I turn aside, I turn about,
And still love beckons, burning bright—
And ever, ever facing me
There hands a sword that men call Right.

I fight the battle in my heart,
And wavering is the victory;
And then I pray to God for strength,
In this, my own Gethsemane.

Oft in my agony of soul
I wonder if God hears my prayers,
And—may He now forgive the thought—
I sometimes wonder if God cares.

The Class of '94

O muse assist me while I sing.
In poetry and rhyme;
The deeds and exploits of a class,
The greatest of its time.

The greatest, yes the greatest,
That has trodden A. U. ground;
The equal of which never has,
And never will be found.

So long as old A.U. shall stand,
May it forever more;
You shall always hear the praises,
Of the class of '94.

To tell the separate virtues,
Of each one of this band;
Would take more time and paper,
Than I have now at hand.

So I'll simply call the name of each
And very briefly tell;
The noble traits of character,
For which he's known so well.

There is our calculator,
For mathematics fame,
He's known throughout the world abroad,
"Old Newton" is his name.

He calculates the weight of worlds,
He can calculate the time;
'Twould take to teach an elephant,
A greasy pole to climb.

An electric engineer he is,
But 'twas a funny sight,
To see him once try to blow out,
An incandescent light.

There's Coffea of judicial fame,
He has much brain 'tis said;
I think you would conclude the same,
By looking at his head.

He makes new friends yes every week,
And walks them down the street,
Invites them in a restaurant,
And makes them stand the treat.

But he's the "ONLY" in the class,
He's always "up to snuff";
But do not let him scare you,
For he's mighty on the bluff.

Then next comes cowboy Hodges,
He is one of the "best";
When first he came among us
He was a terror from the West.

A sixteen shooter in his belt,
A razor in his hand;
He looked the very leader,
Of some hostile Texas band.

But now he's softening down a bit,
I think that it is due;
To a maiden who lives across the bridge,
Yes I'm sure that's true.

Old Gamma, one of Africa's sons,
He's planning what is right;

To go back to his native land,
And take the gospel light.

This is no joke, 'tis very true,
He can't plain English speak;
But he's away up "out of sight,"
When it comes to getting Greek.

Of evangelic turn is Strip,
The day is not so far;
When he'll be known thro' out the land,
As a pulpit orator.

Sam Jones will be no circumstance,
Sam Small will be quite small;
Stripling will loom up like a tower,
The greatest of them all.

He'll preach from East to Golden Gate,
From Great Lakes to the Gulf;
There's only one thing bad he'll do,
He will buy goods from Wolfe.

There's Howard known to baseball time,
As, First Base King, you know,
And when it comes to playing there
He's nothing very slow.

He's Grace itself upon the bag,
And handles with all ease;
The swiftest ball that you might throw,
As though 'twere made of cheese.

And "Fesser Ben," the brilliant
Who gets lessons without toil;
Through every night till half past two,
He burns the midnight oil.

The "Fesser" he is quite sedate,
'Tis in his line you know,
To go about so dignified,
And walk so very slow.

Now comes along old Parson Jack,
That's not his name by far;
Because I think before he'll preach,
He'll run a little bar.

Why he is called the Parson,
Is a puzzle still to me;
For Jack he says he'll never preach,
He'll swear it on his "B."

There's Towns who wears the pompadour,
An orator he'll rise;
See with what case he pocketed,
The famous Quiz Club prize.

And when it comes to catching ball,
There are no flies on him;
He stands behind the bat and says,
"Just let them come on Jim."

He holds down "Jim's most deadly curves"
The in shoot and the rise;
With ease and grace that certainly,
Would cause you some surprise.

Lastly, but not least comes Dr. Nat,
Of fluent tongue he is;
Although to the surprise of all,
He got left on the "Quiz."

The Dr. is quietly learned,
I really think he knows;

The quickest and the safest cure,
For bleeding of the nose.

Now when it comes to talking,
The Dr. is not "slow";
When conversation lulls with him,
The rest had better go.

He'll talk about the weather,
He'll ask, where will it rain;
He'll ask you that just twenty times
Then ask you once again.

But, he'll also talk on science,
On literature and art;
Whenever it comes to talking,
He can always have my part.

Now there is one I will not name,
Pen cannot him describe;
He hopes he'll ne'er forgotten be,
He is your humble scribe.

Grandmother's Bible

I have many costly volumes bound in velvet and in gold,
Old and rare which I've collected far and wide;
But there's not one which I cherish like the Bible worn and old,
Given me by my grandmother when she died.
She called me to her bedside, she kissed me and she said,
Keep this boy forever near your heart;
Not sparkling, glittering diamonds, nor in the want of bread,
Can tempt me with that dear old book to part.

Refrain.
Grandmother's Bible, Grandmother's Bible;
It through life has ever been my guide;
I have many costly volumes, but above them all I prize,
The Bible which she gave me when she died.

II

It is stained with many tear drops and her fingers mark each
    page,
Yet not one of those dear marks I care to hide;
For they make it still more precious and my love shall grow
    with age,
For the Bible which she gave me when she died.
On life's dark, stormy ocean it has been my beacon light,
When waves rolled high and all hope seemed no more;
In old age's beautiful waters with haven just in sight,
It is my pilot to the better shore.

A Dream

I dreamed of you last night, love,
And the dream was one of bliss,
You softly stole upon me,
On my lips you pressed a kiss.
A kiss so soft and gentle,
It seemed, some being of love
Had touched my lips with perfume,
Gathered from heaven above.
It gently eased my weary heart,
It cooled my fevered brain,
It felt what seems must be the joy
Of a flower after rain.
I woke, yes truly thinking,
Your own sweet face to meet;
But found it only just a dream,
A dream so wondrous sweet.
O, why should dreams be fleeting?
Why do they die at birth?
For they mingle the joys of heaven,
With these transient joys of earth.

Sonnet

My heart be brave, and do not falter so,
Nor utter more that deep, despairing wail.
Thy way is very dark and drear I know,
But do not let thy strength and courage fail;
For certain as the raven-winged night
Is followed by the bright and blushing morn,
Thy coming morrow will be clear and bright;
'Tis darkest when the night is furthest worn.
Look up, and out, beyond, surrounding clouds,
And do not in thine own gross darkness grope,
Rise up, and casting off thy hind'ring shrouds,
Cling thou to this, and ever inspiring hope:
    Tho' thick the battle and tho' fierce the fight,
    There is a power making for the right.

Sonnet—The Secret

O could I send my spirit out to her,
To tell the sweetest secret of my heart,
The secret which it can no longer hear
But still with which it is so loth to part.
Or could I give it to some sighing wind,
To softly whisper it within her ear;
Or to some little fairy good and kind,
Who would on wings of love my secret hear.
Could I but tell it to her with my eyes,
And I breathe it deeply in upon her soul,
Would she but read within a lover's sighs,
The passion I no longer can control.
Ah, no, to such frail hopes too long I've clung.
I'll tell myself and do it with my tongue.

Class Poem

Once in a far and distant age,
So tells the ancient fable page,
Were seven sages wise and old:
Of whom a wondrous tale is told.

'Twas said a time there had been when
They were but wise as other men,
And that their skill was due above
To having touched a magic stone,
Which gave to them the secrets deep
That only gods are wont to keep.

Long had the virtues of this stone
In legendary tale been known,
Full many a bard had sung its praise
Full many a minstrel in his lays
Had told the story o'er and o'er
About its magic power.

But few would even for its sake
The perilous journey undertake;
For this the ancient legend ran
About this marv'lous talisman.

Far, far toward the flaming East
Where Phoebus breaks his nightly rest,
Far o'er a vast untrodden plain
Where never falls the dewy rain,
But where the sun's bright, scorching rays
Are blinding to the traveler's gaze.
And where as far as eye can see
He sees no trace of mortal man,
The traveler must go.
Beyond the lofty mountain brow
Enrobed in an eternal snow,

And where the wind's cold, chilling blast
Shrieks thro' the caverns deep and vast.

Where in a dark and gloomy cave
Three hundred-headed monsters rave,
· And shake the mountain in their rage;
For nought their anger can assuage.

And having passed the mountain height
And reached the other side aright,
At length the traveler must embark
Across a river deep and dark.
O'er which there hangs by night and day
A fog, thro' which no single ray
Of light can ever penetrate
This gloomy food to illuminate.
And having reached the other side,
(should he escape the seething tide)
He still must wend his weary way
Towards the cradle of the day.

At last with toil and travel worn
He'll reach the rosy gates of morn,
But, here before these portals bright
Two dragons guard by day and night.
If these are passed the way thou lies
Beneath the blue (ethereal) skies,
Which fair Aurora's blushing cheek
Is wont with crimson tints to streak.
And into an ambrosial wood,
Where long the golden shrine has stood
Upon whose altar long has shown
The wondrous, gleaming magic stone,
Which if tis touched by human hand
He who has touched will understand
The hidden mysteries of Fate
And every secret small and great.
But once tis touched its light will fade

Its gleaming eye be rayless made,
Its charm will be forever lost
One touch its virtue will exhaust.

These seven men had heard this tale,
And well-determined not to fail,
They set out with a stalwart band
To seek this far and distant land.

A while they all befit on their way
With cheerful hearts and spirits gay,
For until now their way had been
This meadow, and o'er fields of green.
But soon they reached the desert plain,
Where never falls the dewy rain,
And here the sun with all his main
Beamed fiercely down upon the train.
Then many sore discouraged grew,
And turning, traced their steps anew.

The others journeyed on until
They reached that steep and rugged hill.
Whose summit mounts up to the stars,
Where speed the gods their winged cars,
And Jove his potent thunder hurls
And blazing coils of fire uncurls.

To climb this bare and barren peak
Taxed the endurance of the weak.
And one by one they backward fell,
What was their fate no one can tell.
Those who could scale this barren clift
And bear the chilling, wintry drift,
The raging monsters in their cave,
And all the other terrors brave,
Arrived at last at that dark stream
That borders on the earth's extreme,

Which they must cross the prize to gain
Or else their journey was in vain.

And many, tho' they bore the pain,
And suffering of the desert plain,
Altho' they sealed the rugged height
And braved the tempest in its might,
Now paused and trembled to behold
This murky stream so dark and cold.

The others boldly entered in,
Resolved the cherished prize to win,
And tho' they struggled hard and long
Against the current swift and strong,
But seven reached the other side:
The rest had perished in the tide.

The seven bravely journeyed on
Towards the fountains of the sun.
Before the gates of morn they drew,
The guarding dragons quickly slew,
And entered the ambrosial wood
Wherein the golden temple stood,
Upon whose altar all alone,
Resplendent lay the magic stone.
They kneeled around the burning flame,
Reward for all their toils to claim,
And at the giving of the wood
Each touched the stone with one accord.
There instantly its mystic light
Grew red and infinitely bright.
Then slowly died its fiery glow
Till nought brightness did it show,
But, quicker than the lightning flash,
Seen across a stormy sky to dash
More rapid than a thought can find
Its passage thro' the human mind,

To them as round the shrine they kneeled
The depths of knowledge were revealed.
They knew the future as the past,
Each mystery however cast;
For to the preserving seven
The minds of gods had there been given.

Not long ago another band
Set out to reach a distant land,
This was the purpose held in mind,
A greater talisman to find.
A talisman whose burning light
Remains forever clear and bright,
The more 'tis touched it brighter grows
And far more clear the light it shows,
The longer there the touch remains
The more the power that it gains.

But since this band set out that day
Many have fallen by the way.
Some, when they reached the sun-burnt plain
Grew faint-hearted and returned again.
Some others journeyed on until,
They reached that steep and rugged hill.
Those who have dared the foaming tide
And reached aright the other side,
Now stand inside the shining gate
And just before the temple wait.
They catch the fragrance of the trees
And it is borne upon the breeze,
There stands before them just in sight
The talisman so clear and bright
May each one enter at the door.
God bless the class of '94.

Voluptas (II)

Pleasure, the drink by which the gods
Make suffering more keen.
A fleeting paradise of fools
Who're dazzled in its sheen.

'Tis but a day that dulls the sense
To present pain and grief,
That fashions dreams whose wildest flights
Of bliss are only brief.
'Tis but an effervescent draught
That sparkles in the light,
But loses all its glitter at
The first approach of night.

To surfeit till the appetite
Grows sickened at the feast,
But still to feel the stinging pangs
Of hunger more increased.
To drain the cup to its last dregs
With mad, delirious joy.
But still to feel the burning thirst
Which it cannot destroy.
The bright mirage one chases o'er
The hot and burning sands,
And dies with thirst while gazing on
The green and shaky strands.

Optimistic Sam

Times am hard and money is
   As scarce as scarce can be.
I got no job. I got no chance
   But it all de same to me.

I ain't worrying myself
   About de way things seem
I takes life jis de way it comes
   I finds it heap more fun.

Once I had an easy job
   Working on Broadway,
Jes a little work each day
   For which I used to draw my pay.
I lost dat job. I got dead broke
   I don't know who's to blame.
Been looking now for six long months
   But I's living jes de same.

Time is hard and money is as scarce
   As de hair upon a flea.
And dat ain't all it's even scarcer
   Dan dat wid me.
What wuz and is and is to be
   I never lets it worry me.
If de sky is clear and long comes de rain
   I ain't gon try to stop it by working my brain.
I keep my mind from troubles free
   Dat is my philosophy.

De good book says dat everything
   Will come to dem dat wait.
I believe de something and I'm satisfied
   For to git mine at dat rate.

Mobile Mardi Gras

Have you heard the news?
There's no time to lose,
If you've got the "Blues"
Get your baggage ready.
Take a friendly tip,
And you'll make a trip,
Down to a southern town, not far away.

Maybe you have seen,
Pictures on the screen
Of the Carnival in Venice;
No need to go there,
You can see it here
Down in Mobile,
Down in Mobile, Alabama.

You will wear a smile,
For each railroad mile;
That you travel down to Dixie,
Where the folks have hearts,
Warmer than the weather.

So then clear the way,
We are off today,
For old Mobile
For old Mobile, Alabama.

After My First Week Teaching in the Country

O could I bid some genie,
To bear me far away,
Where I might get a good square meal,
And red-bugs have no sway.

True, I get lots to eat and drink,
But oh, it is so rough;
When I get hold of something nice,
I can hardly get enough.

But there these pies and "tater poons,"
When they are made up right
Leave old man Cox's "iron clads,"
Away back "out of sight."

The biscuits—O well, I suppose,
They have their uses, for,
What splendid bombs and cannon balls,
They'd make in case of war.

But with their properties as food,
I would not like to fool;
For from their looks I really think,
They'd kill a Texas mule.

It is the job of jobs to teach,
A colored country school;
I almost side with men who say,
The negro is a fool.

He never seems to understand,
A simple thing that is said;
Oh! if there is anything opaque
It is a "nigger's" head.

I tire of country scurry,
I tire of hog and greens;
I'd rather eat on A.U. bull,
And take in city scenes.

These country dudes and dudesses,
They make me feel so dull;
I'd think myself in clover now,
To sport the old "mogul."

O, give me back my city-life,
And everything it means;
E'en though I board at old A.U.
And weekly dine on beans.

To a Brook Near My School House

Thou winding silvery thread,
Finding thy hidden way;
Through foliage dense and green,
Stop, list to what I say.

Tell me, where can I find,
The joy which is thine own:
With which you course your way,
With never, never a moan?

Thou seem'st to laugh so gay,
To catch the bright sun-beam;
As stealing through the trees it comes,
To kiss thy rippling stream.

Thy gurgling music seems,
To give me some faint touch;
Of the joy which is thine own,
O how I long for such.

O tell me, can in truth,
Such joy be found? I seem
To hear the answer, "No,
Save 'neath my cooling stream."

A Recollection

In the trees the birds were singing,
And the winds were sighing faint;
Every breeze sweet perfume bringing,
Everything with sweetness taint.

In the parlor they were dancing,
Singing, talking, laughing free;
But to us far more entrancing,
Was love's low, sweet melody.
And the twilight hour nearing,
Hush the music of the birds;
But to me far, far more churning,
Was the music of your words.

Ever more shall I remember,
How you looked that evening fair;
At the day's last dying ember,
'Neath the parlor window there.

The Last Waltz

Among treasured recollection,
There is one among the few;
Which brings tender, sweet reflections,
'Tis that last, sweet waltz with you.

As we timed its dreamy measure,
Floating as if on air;
In the highest realms of pleasure,
With no thought of pain or care.

While the happy moments fleeing,
To music of no earthly theme;
How I longed to pass my being,
In that one sweet blissful dream.

And your soft hands' gentle pleasure,
Ah, I seem to feel it still;
Filled my soul to utmost measure,
With a wild, ecstatic thrill.

And the fragrance of your flowers,
As soft, delicate and light;
As though plucked from heavenly bowers,
Lingered with me all that night.

How my soul was filled with rapture,
As you raised your eyes to mine;
And my heart yielded in capture
To your heavenly look, divine.

Till my heart beats its last measure,
Till this fleeting life flow halts,
Long as mem'ry holds a treasure,
Shall I cherish that last waltz.

To a Friend

Many sad hearts may you lighten,
And turn sorrow oft to bliss;
Many dark lives may you brighten,
If you'll make your motto this:
"Ever lend a helping hand."

Only Trust Me

What today is dark with sorrow,
Will be bright with joy tomorrow;
Only trust me.
All the gloomy days will brighten,
All the heavy clouds will lighten;
Only trust me.
Time will draw aside the curtain,
From what now is but uncertain;
Only trust me.
Not the things which seem believing,
What we see is oft deceiving;
Only trust me.
But forgetting all past sorrow,
Waiting patiently the 'morrow;
Only trust me.

A Brand

He wandered through the earth despised,
Condemned of men;
Hunted was he from every cave,
And sheltering den.

Upon his brow he wore a brand,
And on his back;
A thousand stripes for it he bore:
His skin was black.

One day he stood at Heaven's gate,
His toil was o'er;
He entered, stood before his God.
His soul was pure.

Christmas Carol

Hail! O hail thee! lovely morn'
Jesus Christ our Lord is born;
Joy, the holy angels cry,
Joy through earth, through air and sky.
See His star in heaven appear,
Hosts of angels hovering near;
Guide me to the Holy Lamb,
Lowly Babe of Bethlehem.
Hark to the angelic strains,
Song prevails and music reigns;
Rise, sons of men and join the choir,
Sing, while archangels strike the lyre;
Let the gladsome news resound,
Man's redemption now is found;
Man is saved forever more,
Let it sound from shore to shore.
Peal it forth ye merry bells,
Over hills, through glades, through dells;
Let the air with gladness ring,
Heavens and earth together sing;
Sing of man's redeemed estates,
Of God's love so deep, so great,
Swell the chorus o'er again,
Peace on earth, good will toward men.

Miserable

Miserable, miserable, weary of life,
Worn with turmoil, its dim and its strife,
And with its burden of grief,
Miserable, miserable.

Feeling my life one great error has been,
Filled to its full with the dark dregs of sin;
And all the woe which that brings,
Miserable, miserable.

Weary and heartsick I seek, but in vain,
A friend to share my sorrow and pain;
But there is no friend for me,
Miserable, miserable.

Yet 'tis an end but righteous and just,
Little do I deserve friendship and trust;
Let all my sorrow be mine,
Miserable, miserable.

Deeply I drink from the thrice bitter bowl,
Feeling the iron entering my soul;
With all its bitterest pangs;
Miserable, miserable.

To H.B.

Ever may your life be bright,
Strong in battling for the right;
Trampling down the wrong.
Ever helping all in need,
Lending aid in word and deed;
Lifting those not strong.

To a Friend, with a Rose

Violet, Violet,
Take this rose with dew-drops wet,
Pledge that thee I'll ne'er forget,
Violet, sweet Violet.

A Heathen

I am a heathen poor and blind,
I have no cultured, polished mind,
In me no talents rare you'll find,
Only a poor heathen.

My way is dark, I cannot see,
No beacon light shines out for me,
It must beneath some bushes be,
O who will help the heathen?

I wander thro' the earth alone,
By no one sought, by no one known,
No tender deeds to me are shown,
No one can love a heathen.

Wherever I should chance to be,
The Christians always point at me,
And say a heathen man is he,
A poor benighted heathen.

My hands are neither deft nor skilled.
My mind has not been trained and drilled,
And with rich stores of nonsense filled,
A poor unlearned heathen.

I do not know that art so great,
Of showing as I glibly prate,
The contents of my hollow pate,
O pity the poor heathen.

I think that I shall go to school,
And learn to be a learned fool,
At least know as much as a mule,
And be no more a heathen.

To My Valentine

Let others have what earth can give,
Rich treasures boundless as the sea;
For me it is enough to live,
To love you and be cared by thee.

Ode to Florida

Florida, fair Florida, land of my birth,
Queen of the continent, gem of the earth.
Land where the skies are blue as the sea,
Where the bright laughing waters are flowing and free.
Land of fair sunlight,
Land of soft starlight,
Land where the moon is queen of the night,
I love thee, I love thee with passionate love.

Thou liest wrapped in the ocean's arms,
Old Neptune feasts upon thy charms,
And runs to kiss thy coral shore,
As a lover speeds to his lady's bower.
Beautiful Florida!
Lovely Florida!
Most favored spot of a favored land.

Sweet land of sweet flowers,
Of soft summer showers,
I love all thy plains, all thy rivers and lakes.
I love all thy forests, thy marshes and brakes,
Every slow-winding creek,
That flows on to seek
A path to the rivers and thence to the sea,
Is loved by me, fondly loved by me.

The noble St. Johns, thy boast and thy pride,
How my heart flows along on its ceaseless tide,
As in majesty flowing,
Flowing, flowing,
It comes from the far, far south to be
Mingled at last with the great open sea.

And that dream of a stream,
The Ocklawaha,

Flowing serene,
Through a tropical scene,
Where the sleepy-eyed saurian basks in the sunlight,
And the bright-hued flamingo stalks in the moonlight,
Where the mosses hang low from the cypress trees,
And the golden fruit sways in the autumn breeze.
How dear to my heart, my fond heart.

And thy huge Everglades stretching out like a sea,
Brooding in silence and mystery,
Wrapped in mystery,
Death-like mystery,
Vast and unknown as the fathomless sea,
Is reverenced by me, held in reverence by me.

O, land of my birth, be the land of my death.
May I draw 'neath thy skies my last fleeting breath,
May my grave be beneath the moss-covered trees,
My requiem sounded by thy tropic seas,
As they beat on the shore,
Evermore.

Acknowledgment

Your simple words:
Our feelings should not be our guide
Have done for me
What hours and days of thought could not.
I've racked my brain
To know what step I next should take,
But now I see my duty plain
And clear; laid out before me like
A straight and even, well-made road.
Which leads me out from all this doubt
Of what is right for me to do.

I now can see
How that the passions of my heart
So long pent up, when given vent
Rose like a mist to cloud my brain,
And made me so unfit to think.
I could not think, decide or act,
But all my sense seemed in a whirl
And when my reason urged me
To do the right, some foolish thought
Sprang from my heart and told me, No.
And now I know the foulest foe
To reason, one that renders blunt
The edge and keenness of the mind,
Is the hot passion of the heart.
'Tis but too true,
Men's passions often make them look
And do what, in their minds,
They would condemn,
And what you add—"Just for my sake"
Now makes my duty far more sweet.

It is not now an irksome task
I must perform without reward.
For my reward comes in the act
Of doing what you wish.

The Passionate Lover

Cold blows the north wind, bleak and strong,
Wild beat the waves upon the shore;
The tempest howls, the surges roar,
And from the angry ocean wide,
In flows the restless, white-crowned tide,
O'er the whole night long.

Cold blows the north wind bleak and strong,
The billows in delirious glee,
Roll in from 'cross the foaming sea;
And in their mad and merry race,
They fling the salt spray in my face,
And chant their dreary song.

The wind is fierce, the sea is bold,
But what care I for wind or sea;
What terrors has the storm for me!
I love; and in my heart there burns,
A flame that sea and tempest spurns,
A flame that fears not cold.

My heart's aflame, my blood aboil,
With love, with all the fires of love;
These cold winds circling me above,
And sweeping 'cross the briny flow,
But fan the flame, and make it glow,
Like fires fed with oil.

I dare that Tempest in thy might,
My love shall never suffer harms;
To shield her from the beating storm
I'll bare my naked breast to thee,
Thou cruel, harsh, unfeeling sea,
All thro' the dreary night.

Cling to me, Love, still closer cling,
My strong arms folded round thy form,
Thou needst not fear the sea, the storm,
But why is thy embrace so weak?
Canst thou not trust to me, Love, speak,
To brave the fierce Storm King?

Or art thou cold and passionless?
Then let my life blood's fervid flow,
Kindle love's fires and make them glow,
Until thy melting heart, once cold,
Feels all the joys of love untold;
Feels love's true happiness.

And let me look into thine eyes,
And press my warm heart close to thine;
Drink from thy lips the honeyed wine,
'Til I am drunkened with the bliss;
That flows free from a lover's kiss,
That in love's embrace lies.

Let me thy still affections move,
Let me thy slumbering passions wake;
'Til love doth full possession take,
Let me melt down thine icy heart,
And teach to the air Love's sweet art,
Teach to thee how to Love.

My Love, by yonder bending sky,
By yonder weary, moaning sea;
By all these winds so wild and free,
By all beneath, by all above,
Thou art my life, my soul, my love:
No lover loves as I.

And yet sayst thou it cannot be?
Hast thou no kinder word for me?

For tho' I fear not wind or sea;
Tho' I dread not the tempest bold.
I cannot bear a love so cold.

Such love would quench the flame divine;
That burns on cupid's sacred shrine:—
Winds, blow me to some resting place.
Cold Lea, I come to thy embrace,
My love is lost to me.

Art vs. Trade

Trade, Trade versus Art,
Brain, Brain versus Heart;
Oh, the earthiness of these hard-hearted times,
When clinking dollars, and jingling dimes,
Drown all the finer music of the soul.

Life as an Octopus with but this creed,
That all the world was made to serve his greed;
Trade has spread out his mighty myriad claw,
And drawn into his foul polluted maw,
The brightest and the best,
Well nigh,
Has he drained dry,
The sacred fount of Truth;
And if, forsooth,
He has left yet some struggling streams from it to go,
He has contaminated so their flow,
That Truth, scarce is it true.

Poor Art with struggling gasp,
Lies strangled, dying in his mighty grasp;
He locks his grimy fingers 'bout her snowy throat so tender.
Is there no power to rescue her, protect, defend her?
Shall Art be left to perish?
Shall all the images her shrines cherish
Be left to this iconoclast, to vulgar Trade?

Oh, that mankind had less of Brain and more of Heart,
Oh, that the world had less of Trade and more of Art;
Then would there be less grinding down the poor,
Then would men learn to love each other more;
For Trade stalks like a giant through the land,
Bearing aloft the rich in his high hand,
While down beneath his mighty ponderous tread,
He crushes those who cry for daily bread.

The Poet's Harp

My harp is hushed,
It will not sing to me;
The soft and pleasing song,
Its erstwhile song.
I take it down,
And softly draw my hands,
Across the strings, but still,
It does not answer to
My ling'ring touch.

My heart is sad,
Because my harp is mute;
For when it sang to me,
It thrilled my inmost soul,
And gave to me a joy,
I cannot tell.

It was my life,
When listening to its songs,
I bent an eager ear,
To catch its softest note,
Which none but me could hear—
'Twas but for me.

It sang to me,
To fit my ev'ry mood;
When I was sad and drear,
Its tones were low and sweet,
And were a soothing balm,
To all my grief.

To set my cheeks aglow,
And make my blood
Go dancing through my veins
In ecstasy.

But now 'tis hushed,
I put it by, and loath,
I take a sad farewell,
To all the joys that once
It gave to me.

I Love Thee Still

I loved thee once, I love thee still,
My heart is yet thine own;
Thou art its sole and rightful queen,
It is thy royal throne.

What though dark fate between us stands,
And clouds between us roll;
Not clouds, not even fate can stay
The flight of soul to soul.

No power upon the earth below,
Nor none in heaven above;
Time nor eternity can break
The golden chain of love.

To Louie (I)

Louie, Louie, little dear,
Louie, Louie, don't you hear!
Don't hold the cat up by her tail;
Its strength might of a sudden fail.
There, Oh, what a pity!
You would have a little kitty,
Wandering all around forlorn;
Of her pride and beauty shorn,
And not knowing what to do,
But sit alone and mew;
For like a ship without a sail,
Would be a cat without a tail.

A Fragment (I)

And the winds were drearily moaning,
As if chanting some weird requiem;
And the trees were bending and groaning,
And seemed trembling each stalk and each stem.

Untitled Poem

Was what you thought love, but passing,
Was it but an idle dream,
But the passion of a moment,
But a bubble on the stream?

Has my lofty ideal fallen,
Do my hopes all shattered lay;
Have I loved once, and then in vain,
Has my idol turned to clay?

Have you won my heart for conquest,
But to cast it off when won;
And to end my bliss so quickly,
When I thought it just begun?

No, I cannot judge you harshly,
Tho' bitter thoughts my heart now fill,
For with all your faults and failings,
Yet, my own, I love you still.

Untitled Poem

Come with me my love and wander,
Where the moon is shining bright;
And the stars in beauteous splendor,
Softly shed their silv'ry light.
Where the nightingale is singing,
His soft blithesome melody,
And each breeze sweet perfume bringing,
I'll whisper words of love to thee.

FOR THE BEST IN PAPERBACKS, LOOK FOR THE

In every corner of the world, on every subject under the sun, Penguin represents quality and variety—the very best in publishing today.

For complete information about books available from Penguin—including Puffins, Penguin Classics, and Arkana—and how to order them, write to us at the appropriate address below. Please note that for copyright reasons the selection of books varies from country to country.

In the United Kingdom: Please write to *Dept. EP, Penguin Books Ltd, Bath Road, Harmondsworth, West Drayton, Middlesex UB7 0DA.*

In the United States: Please write to *Penguin Putnam Inc., P.O. Box 12289 Dept. B, Newark, New Jersey 07101-5289* or call 1-800-788-6262.

In Canada: Please write to *Penguin Books Canada Ltd, 10 Alcorn Avenue, Suite 300, Toronto, Ontario M4V 3B2.*

In Australia: Please write to *Penguin Books Australia Ltd, P.O. Box 257, Ringwood, Victoria 3134.*

In New Zealand: Please write to *Penguin Books (NZ) Ltd, Private Bag 102902, North Shore Mail Centre, Auckland 10.*

In India: Please write to *Penguin Books India Pvt Ltd, 11 Panchsheel Shopping Centre, Panchsheel Park, New Delhi 110 017.*

In the Netherlands: Please write to *Penguin Books Netherlands bv, Postbus 3507, NL-1001 AH Amsterdam.*

In Germany: Please write to *Penguin Books Deutschland GmbH, Metzlerstrasse 26, 60594 Frankfurt am Main.*

In Spain: Please write to *Penguin Books S. A., Bravo Murillo 19, 1° B, 28015 Madrid.*

In Italy: Please write to *Penguin Italia s.r.l., Via Benedetto Croce 2, 20094 Corsico, Milano.*

In France: Please write to *Penguin France, Le Carré Wilson, 62 rue Benjamin Baillaud, 31500 Toulouse.*

In Japan: Please write to *Penguin Books Japan Ltd, Kaneko Building, 2-3-25 Koraku, Bunkyo-Ku, Tokyo 112.*

In South Africa: Please write to *Penguin Books South Africa (Pty) Ltd, Private Bag X14, Parkview, 2122 Johannesburg.*